The Collapse of the Concert of Europe

International Politics, 1890–1914

RICHARD LANGHORNE
Fellow of St John's College, Cambridge

The signal fires of warning
They blaze, but none regard;
And on through night till morning
The world runs ruinward

A E Housman
(*More Poems*, XLIII)

First edition 1981
Reprivted 1983

Published by
THE MACMILLAN PRESS LTD
London and Basingstoke
Companies and representatives throughout
the world

ISBN 0–333–29211–1
ISBN 0–333–29213–8 (pbk)

Printed in Hong Kong

Contents

The illustration on the front of the book shows the signing of the Treaty of Peace between Turkey and the Balkan States at St James's Palace on 30 May 1913, and is reproduced by kind permission of the Illustrated London News Photographic Library. This peace treaty was made possible by the work of a conference of the London Ambassadors of the five great powers, which had met since December 1912 under the chairmanship of Sir Edward Grey, the British Foreign Secretary. This conference was the last example of the Concert of Europe in action.

FOR HELEN

Foreword

This book is designed to show the working of the principal aspects of international politics, 1890–1914, in a thematic way. It does not seek to give merely a narrative account, nor does it attempt to rely only upon a repetition and summing up of the most modern work specifically upon Germany – though that is a very important theme. It is also necessary to identify and describe other significant factors which were working to destroy the structure of international relations as they had developed since 1815. The development of the Concert of Europe during the nineteenth century had produced the most successful system for regulating international politics that has yet been devised, and in discovering why it collapsed during the period under discussion, substantial clues towards an explanation of the outbreak of war in 1914 emerge.

The themes which are discussed cover the emergence of a non-European sphere of international politics, reaching a crisis point in the Far East at the turn of the century; the effects of a change in the distribution of power occurring in Germany's favour, thus rendering her domestic condition of more than usual significance, as also that of her ally Austria–Hungary; the consequences of the technological and demographic changes of the period, particularly upon communication, weaponry, and the way in which advanced states were coming to be governed. The latter part of the book shows how the general uneasiness and some specific anxieties induced by these developments evoked observable responses from governments, responses which though in some ways were designed to buttress, in fact set in train a gradual collapse of the Concert of Europe. Finally, these developments and responses coincided in their effects and resulted in the failure of states to control the crisis of 1914. This process is described in the last chapter of the book.

I am deeply grateful for the help I have received in writing this book from Professor Maurice Larkin of the University of Edinburgh, Professor F. H. Hinsley, Master of St John's College, Cambridge, Professor

F. S. L. Lyons, Provost of Trinity College, Dublin and Professor Geoffrey Warner of the University of Leicester. I would not have written this book without the encouragement and constant questioning of several generations of history students at the University.of Kent, and although it is too large a number to name each individually, I am grateful to them all.

Cambridge 1980   R. T. B. L.

Map Section

List of Maps

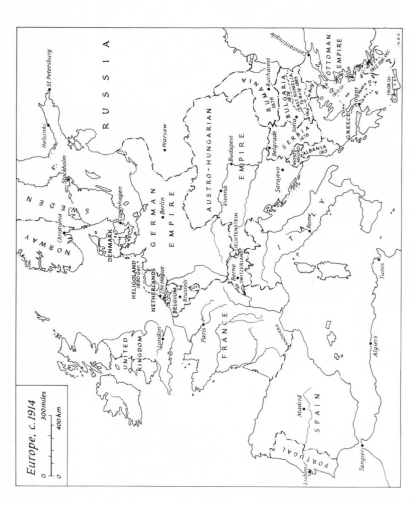

Europe, c. 1914

Map 1

x

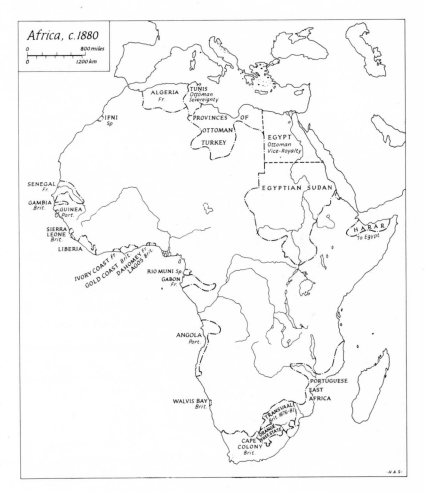

Africa, c.1880

0   800 miles
0   1200 km

ALGERIA
Fr.

TUNIS
Ottoman
Sovereignty

IFNI
Sp

PROVINCES   OF

OTTOMAN

TURKEY

EGYPT
Ottoman
Vice-Royalty

EGYPTIAN SUDAN

SENEGAL
Fr.

GAMBIA
Brit.

GUINEA
Port.

SIERRA
LEONE
Brit.

LIBERIA

HARAR
To Egypt

IVORY COAST Fr.
GOLD COAST Brit.
DAHOMEY Fr.
LAGOS Brit.

RIO MUNI Sp

GABON
Fr.

ANGOLA
Port.

PORTUGUESE
EAST
AFRICA

WALVIS BAY
Brit.

TRANSVAAL
Brit. 1876-81

ORANGE
FREE STATE

CAPE
COLONY
Brit.

-H.A.S-

Map 2

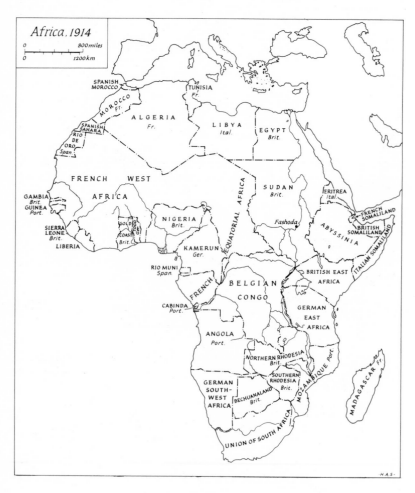

Africa, 1914

0 _____ 800 miles
0 _____ 1200 km

SPANISH MOROCCO

TUNISIA
Fr.

MOROCCO
Fr.

ALGERIA
Fr.

LIBYA
Ital.

EGYPT
Brit.

SPANISH SAHARA

RIO DE ORO
Span.

FRENCH WEST

AFRICA

SUDAN
Brit.

ERITREA
Ital.

FRENCH SOMALILAND

GAMBIA
Brit.
GUINEA
Port.

SIERRA LEONE
Brit.

LIBERIA

GOLD COAST
Brit.

NIGERIA
Brit.

KAMERUN
Ger.

EQUATORIAL AFRICA

Fashoda

ABYSSINIA

BRITISH SOMALILAND

ITALIAN SOMALILAND

RIO MUNI
Span.

FRENCH

BELGIAN

CONGO

BRITISH EAST
AFRICA

CABINDA
Port.

GERMAN

EAST

AFRICA

ANGOLA
Port.

NORTHERN RHODESIA
Brit.

SOUTHERN RHODESIA
Brit.

MOZAMBIQUE Port.

GERMAN
SOUTH-
WEST
AFRICA

BECHUANALAND
Brit.

MADAGASCAR Fr.

UNION OF SOUTH AFRICA

H.A.S.

Map 3

xii

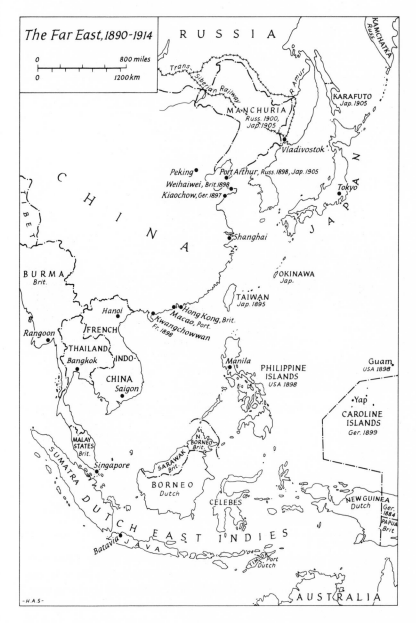

The Far East, 1890-1914

| 0 | | 800 miles |
| 0 | | 1200km |

RUSSIA

KANCHATKA
Russ.

Trans Siberian Railway

Amur

MANCHURIA
Russ. 1900,
Jap. 1905

KARAFUTO
Jap. 1905

Vladivostok

CHINA

TIBET

Peking

Port Arthur, Russ. 1898, Jap. 1905
Weihaiwei, Brit. 1898
Kiaochow, Ger. 1897

JAPAN

Tokyo

Shanghai

OKINAWA
Jap.

BURMA
Brit.

Rangoon

Hanoi

Hong Kong, Brit.
Macao, Port.
Kwangchowwan
Fr. 1898

TAIWAN
Jap. 1895

FRENCH

THAILAND

Bangkok

INDO-
CHINA
Saigon

Manila

PHILIPPINE
ISLANDS
USA 1898

Guam
USA 1898

Yap

CAROLINE
ISLANDS
Ger. 1899

MALAY
STATES
Brit.

Singapore

SARAWAK
Brit.

N.
BORNEO
Brit.

SUMATRA

BORNEO
Dutch

CELEBES

NEW GUINEA
Dutch

Ger.
1884
PAPUA
Brit.

DUTCH EAST INDIES

Batavia JAVA

TIMOR Port.
Dutch

AUSTRALIA

-H.A.S-

Map 4

xiii

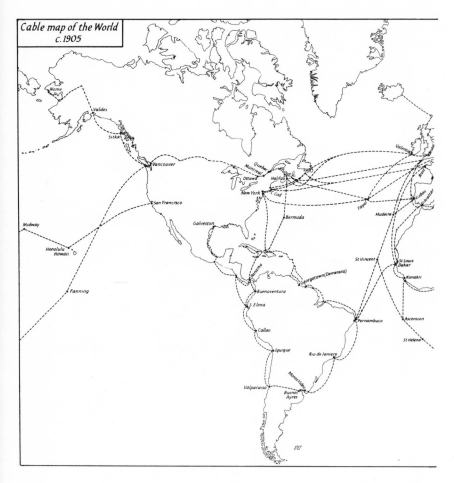

Cable map of the World
c. 1905

Map 5

Note for Map 5

A telegraphic map of 1855 published by the Electric Telegraph
lines outside Europe, except for a temporary submarine cable across
existed to Constantinople, though one was under construction.
No intercontinental telegraph lines had yet been completed. By 1905,
as can be seen from this simplified map, a dramatic improvement had

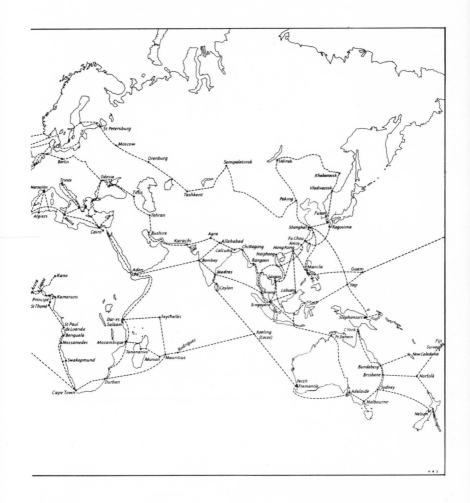

Company and the International Telegraph Company showed no
the Black Sea from Varna to Balaclava in the Crimea. No line yet
Except for Constantinople, all the European capitals were connected.
however, all developed areas were equipped with domestic lines, and,
taken place in intercontinental communications.

PART ONE

The Bases of Insecurity

1. The General Context

Looked at from the last quarter of the twentieth century, the collapse of
the European international system seems to have a fundamentally
straightforward explanation, correctly forecast by de Tocqueville[1] and
others, but obscured by the rise and domination of Germany 1871–1944.
The European international system was unlikely to survive the end of
European primacy and the shift of power to the largest political units in
the world, the United States of America and Russia. The pace of that shift
was slowed and its direction largely concealed by the rise of Germany
and, with that rise, further hidden by an increase rather than a decrease in
the concentration of power in Europe. As this process continued, even
more purely European political questions, clearly to be seen after 1907,
came to dominate the international scene. None the less, the ultimately
controlling factor remained the shift in the base of international power;
for the rise of Germany came, particularly during the Chancellorship of
Bülow and *Weltpolitik*, to be expressed in terms of finding a sure
foundation from which to keep up with the potentiality of Russia and the
plainer and more ebullient fact of the United States. Defeat of Germany in
1918 was not, however, followed by a reorganisation of international
politics along new and more realistic lines – by contrast the period
1919–39 produced a spurious and uncomfortable return to a European-
based international system in the face of the Russian Revolution and
American isolationism. In this curious twilight, European domestic and
foreign policies tended to extremes, perhaps in a desperate attempt to
preserve the primacy of Europe, and Germany found herself possessed of
a second chance to secure her base for future security against the great
continental powers. By the end of the Second World War – more clearly
still by 1949 – a new international system had emerged, greatly confused
by an inimical ideological vocabulary, but essentially that which had
been foreseen 100 years before.

II

If the rise of the super powers and the decline of Europe provide the wider context of international politics before the First World War, the final development of the Concert of Europe provides its more immediate background. Most of the instinctive responses of statesmen in the period were conditioned by their surprisingly common conception of an existing European international system. Even as late as 1912–13 a restricted form of the old Concert mechanism was used to control the effects of the Balkan Wars, and in the 1914 crisis itself those who strove so hard to preserve peace did so within the forms of Concert diplomacy. But by then the old ways survived more by sheer inertia than the conscious will of statesmen, for the conditions which had given rise to the Concert in the first place and had underpinned it for so long had, as will be seen, finally disappeared. Much of the international history of the period 1890–1914 can best be understood as part of the process by which this erosion occurred.

Sometimes the nature of the Concert of Europe seems hard to pin down, because so much of it, and so much of its conspicuous success, was based upon attitudes of mind which led to restrained diplomacy, in the interests of restrained objectives. None the less, these attitudes were based upon a particular understanding of a response to the most fundamental of all facts in international politics, the distribution of power. It was only when the experience of dismantling the Napoleonic Empire was added to a determination not to allow the resumption of the chaotic conditions of the eighteenth century, that the statesmen of Vienna proceeded to base their activities on a correct view of the distribution of power. Not only did they acquire the notion that there was a rough equality among the five greater European states, Russia, Austria, Prussia, France and Britain, they also came to believe that this was not new, had only been interrupted by the career of Napoleon I, and was likely to remain for the foreseeable future. In this circumstance, the interests of all powers were best served by not seeking to change an unalterable status quo (as had been tried during the eighteenth century).[2] Indeed, it appeared that the defence of the status quo represented the wisest policy. In the earliest stages of the post-Vienna world, this policy was expressed in a rigid form and could not survive the changes which, without altering the basic arrangements between states, were bound to occur, and bound to require regulation. In quite a short time, and particularly as a result of the outcome – and the method of solution – of the Belgian crisis in 1830–1, the defence of the status quo was redefined as a general agreement not to allow changes in the existing settlement without the consent of the signatory powers: that is without a form of negotiated agreement, most usually achieved at some kind of meeting. Thus the even distribution of power came to express itself in these notions of commonly accepted restraint.

There was also a second fundamental assumption which underlay the Concert of Europe and this was the notion of a defined area within which the commonly accepted notions of restraint would work. The importance of this can clearly be seen in the careful insistence by Russia in 1815 that Turkey-in-Europe did not fall within such an area, as it can in the reaction of Britain to the question of the future of the Spanish Empire in America. As the century wore on, the question of the defined area gave rise to some important conflicts – the Crimean War, the partition of Africa – and the end of the Concert itself was perhaps most clearly signalled when after 1895 affairs in the Far East induced the breakdown of this essential pre-condition. (See chapter 2.)

Both these factors were destroyed at about the same time and for fundamentally the same reason. When they went, it was certain that the framework of assumptions and customary restraints to which they had given rise would eventually follow. Only the pace of the breakdown was uncertain and in the end it was slower than might have been expected. The corroding agent was a speeding up of the process of technological advance in the most developed societies, leading to an alteration in the very currency of power, as well as to a change in the nature of the state itself. (See chapter 4.) But for all that its complicated effects must be discussed in greater detail, there can be little doubt that it was the nature of German technological prowess that brought about her rise and the consequent end of an equality among the greater states. At the same time, a revolution in transport and communications brought about the collapse of the defined area and the irreversible involvement of European powers in affairs which they could not control. Thus the fate of the Concert of Europe at the hands of these and related developments is the context in which the history of international politics in the period must be seen, and much of what has sometimes seemed difficult to understand acquires a new clarity when seen as being part of a frantic search for security by states which recognised – or perhaps merely felt – the effects of the withdrawal of the genuine collective security given by the old system. (See chapters 5 and 6.)

III

Matters were made more difficult by domestic pressures. All states went through a period of great stress during the later nineteenth century, because of major changes in the structure of their societies and in the character and obligations of their governments. The peculiarly representative function of governments dates from this time and induced a corresponding nervousness of other governments, which was new and foreign to the former pre-conceptions of the great powers of the Concert of Europe. In two states in particular, Austria and Germany, there was a profoundly important connection between domestic pressures and foreign policy such as to provide a link between the darkening quality of international politics and the uneasy conditions within Austria and Germany. Indications of such an interlock came rapidly after 1900, and in 1914 it proved to be decisive. (See chapter 3.) It is, however, insufficient to explain why German and Austrian leaders might have felt impelled to make war as an instrument of domestic policy, and then to believe that to be a full explanation of the events of 1914. Neither the opportunity nor the idea would have occurred without the special conditions prevailing in the international system. Nor is it true to say that the declining security amongst the Powers would necessarily have brought on a great war by itself. International uncertainties induced natural anxieties and thus created a situation in which they would be manipulated. This in turn served to increase the atmosphere of uncertainty: tension became self-generating.

The moment of interlock was vital and not inevitable. Time could have pushed either factor into a new and different phase. To take the most obvious speculation, there might have been a crippling domestic breakdown in Germany or the collapse of the Habsburg Empire might have removed the excuse for a Russo-German war.

However, as things stood in 1914, there was already a vicious circle by which German policy was, as will be seen, both a consequence and a cause of growing international disorder. German foreign policy was also, as a result of internal instability, a weapon of domestic policy. In the final crisis, this proved to be a factor of equal importance with that of the similar problem in Austria–Hungary. By a strangely remote process, it turned out to be the Hungarian problem within the Habsburg Empire that dictated restraint after the assassination of Archduke Francis Ferdinand, and in so doing drew out the crisis so that the impulsions of German policy had time to make their effect. Both features of the crisis were derived from recognisable internal struggles. (See chapter 7.)

But the story of how that situation could arise opens with the breakdown of the Concert of Europe, and the next chapter begins the discussion of that process by examining the destruction of the notion and fact of the defined area within which the European international system worked.

Further Reading

G. Barraclough, *An Introduction to Contemporary History* (Pelican, 1967).

L. Dehio, *The Precarious Balance* (Chatto & Windus, 1963).

F. H. Hinsley, *Power and the Pursuit of Peace* (CUP, 1963).

2. Outside Europe: Africa and the Far East

It has been some time since historians began to attribute less importance to non-European affairs in the history of nineteenth-century international politics. These affairs had largely presented themselves in terms of colonial rivalries in Africa, or imperial disputes along the Indian frontiers, and such matters now seem to have significance more as indicators of other factors than as prime movers. It would, however, be a mistake to allow this change of emphasis to lead to a purely Eurocentric view of the importance or otherwise of non-European areas.[1] In the context of the history of the international system, the Far East, particularly, came to have enormous importance at the end of the nineteenth century not so much for what European powers were doing in the area, though this constitutes an essential link, but for the developments which were independently acquiring their own momentum, beyond the ability of the great powers to halt or control. It was this effect which had such debilitating consequences for the Concert of Europe.[2]

The Concert of Europe depended for its existence upon the experience and will of statesmen and nations. This willingness to respond to experience, particularly that of the eighteenth century, depended in turn upon recognition of the existence of limiting factors deriving from the power-relationship of the greater states. It also depended upon an understood and additional limiting factor, namely an accepted area in which the constraints of the Concert of Europe would operate, and this element in the system has consistently been underplayed in historical treatment. Without such an understanding, neither Britain nor Russia would have accepted that the power-relationship between the great powers was sufficiently equal to underpin a general international system. When, as a result of changes in the distribution of power, the defined area of operation came to be changed, such changes were achieved only with difficulty and in the first case – the Crimean War – by means of a fitful war.

Looked at from this angle, there appear to be three occasions in the course of the nineteenth century when the question of the defined area of the Concert of Europe was at issue, and in the third case, failure to solve the problem was a major contributor to its collapse. These occasions were the Crimean War and its subsequent settlement at the Peace of Paris in 1856; the partition of Africa in the mid-1880s; and the Far-Eastern crisis of 1895–1905. The nature of all these crises was different, only the first and the last sharing a similar cause – the collapse of a previously existing great empire. In the first case the solution was successful; in the second it was arrived at only after damaging difficulties, and in the third, no solution emerged.

It was the opinion of Messrs Sellar and Yeatman that the Crimean War was caused by the Holy Places.

> *The French* thought that the *Holy Places* ought to be guarded (probably against the *Americans*) by *Latin Monks*, while *the Turks*, who owned the Places, thought that they ought to be guarded by *Greek Monks*. *England* therefore quite rightly declared war on *Russia*, who immediately occupied *Roumania*.
> The war was consequently fought in *the Crimea* (near *Persia*). . . .

They also thought that the 'war was exceptionally inevitable and was caused by a number of causes'. With their usual aplomb, these celebrated authors have made themselves historically useful once again.[2] It is indeed odd that the war was fought in the Crimea; it did seem that it had no causes; the Russian occupation of the principalities did appear to be irrelevant.

For by the time that the war actually began in the Crimea, each one of the issues over which it is supposed to have broken out was resolved. The Holy Places had long been consigned to limbo; the Ottoman Empire was quite secure; Russia had apparently abandoned her claims in the principalities first by accepting demands of the other powers expressed in the Vienna Note and then by withdrawing her troops. Only her weak Black Sea fleet remained an objection – and that a specious one – to the settlement of the dispute. This last had at least the interesting result that since it was the only difficulty, the only place that the war could start was at Sevastopol. Austria and Prussia, although they were benevolently neutral, could not in the end bring themselves to fight – certainly not while the British and the French were doing so for them, although in the end they played a considerable part in bringing Russia to accept the terms that were offered her after defeat in battle. The whole affair has a thoroughly unreal air, caught so well in the quotation from *1066 And All That*.[3]

But there are consistent features, despite the behaviour of Napoleon III. It was, for a start, clearly a Russian problem and not a Turkish one. It turned basically upon the old question as to whether Russia should be allowed to arrange and maintain a private agreement with the Turkish Empire by which she would secure a substantial advantage in the race for Balkan territory. The powers had not liked the Treaty of Unkiar Skelessi in 1833, and it had taken them the length of the Mehemet Ali affair to reverse it and substitute the Straits Convention of 1841.[4] Now it looked as if Russian intervention in the form of Prince Menshikov's mission was going to repeat this situation to an even greater effect. There were constant references to the necessity of obtaining a European decision. It was held to be an affair for the Concert; the powers produced the Vienna Note. Even Russell was moved to tell the Russians that partition must mean a conference. The Holy Alliance fell apart before the insoluble problem of the eastern question. The only way of satisfactorily solving, or postponing the solution of, the eastern question was by placing Turkey-in-Europe firmly within the bounds of the European international system. Just after the war had begun formally, the Austrians and the French produced the four points, which were in a sense the war aims, and eventually made up the body of the concluding treaty. Everything by now had been solved, there were no issues left: they had to say for what they were really fighting or supporting the war. The points were:

1. Russian protectorate over provinces to be replaced by a European guarantee.

2. Navigation of the Danube to be free and under European supervision.

3. Straits Convention to be revised in the interests of the balance of power in Europe.

4. Security for the Christians to be guaranteed by the great powers.[5]

To gain Russian consent to these points a war was necessary, and when it was over the victorious powers behaved quite unlike their forebears in such a situation: they made the chief article of the Peace of Paris a point of principle. Turkey-in-Europe was declared to be part of the public law of Europe and the effect of this provision can be clearly seen in the existence and decisions of the Congress of Berlin of 1878.[6]

The extensions of 1856 had partly come about because of the apparently uncheckable decline of the Ottoman Empire, thus leaving the area a tempting source of confusion and possible gain, and partly because there had been a relative change in the positions of France – moved upward by the successful establishment of the Second Empire – and Russia – moved downward by her slower development towards the economic and administrative infrastructure of a modern great power. The next crisis, that in Africa in the 1880s, arose more from European conditions themselves than from indigenous factors that might seem to be equivalent to the decline of Turkey; although it is true that the precise cause of intervention in Africa was to be found in the decline of Tunis and Egypt. That such an opportunity was used to produce a full-scale extension of the Concert of Europe into Africa arose out of the position of Germany after 1879.

The position of Germany in Europe made the conduct of her relations with Russia and Austria peculiarly problematic, since it was plainly desirable that Germany should neither quarrel with nor become exclusively committed to either power. A policy of equal friendship for each, however, was bedevilled by the fact that both powers showed the strongest tendency to mutual hostility over Balkan nationalism, and therefore both to seek the support of other powers, not least that of Germany. Bismarck managed to hold out without committing himself until the great Near-Eastern crisis of 1876–8, but after the Congress of Berlin such a balancing act was no longer possible, and the inevitable agreement with Austria came in 1879. From that time, even more than since 1871, it became Bismarck's policy to produce a general stalemate in international politics. The constraints upon all powers would prevent them from recognising the significance of the constraint imposed upon Germany herself as a result of her agreement with Austria. The laying-down of smoke-screens became a common tactic of Bismarck and amongst the many means that he employed, for a time Africa became foremost.[7] The process probably began when the occupation of Tunis by France, very much at Bismarck's suggestion, unexpectedly produced a serious crisis in Italian domestic affairs, as disappointed Italian empire-builders briefly seemed likely to set up a new and perhaps threatening republic. In the end, in order to salvage something of the notion that Italy was a great power she was admitted to the Austro-German Alliance, and the regime thus buttressed survived to become a restless and eventually traitorous ally.

II

If the occupation of Tunis in 1881 was one of the causes of the Triple Alliance – albeit indirectly – it was also a foretaste of European activity in northern Africa which was to provide Bismarck with further means for creating smoke-screens to conceal German insecurity. More precisely, the occupation of Egypt in 1882 by Britain made it possible to use consequent Anglo-French hostility to achieve three objects: to issue warnings to Britain; to extend the isolation of France; and to further Franco-German accord. The outcome was an astonishing achievement: France was divided from Britain by the Egyptian question; Britain semi-permanently divided from Russia by Indian ambitions; Russia tied by the Three Emperors' League of 1881; and a new and delightful hold over Britain was presented by international control of the Egyptian debt. It was as near a perfect European system as Germany could want or Bismarck devise – except that it was as difficult to defend as it had been to create.

Nevertheless the occupation presented further opportunities to Bismarck to cloud real international issues in the interests of his policy. His success in this and his acute understanding of the potential divisiveness of colonial rivalries, has masked its significance as a factor in the declining quality of international politics after the scramble for Africa in 1884–5. Imperialism, nationalism and capitalism are the three 'isms' which have been widely credited singly or in combination with bringing on the First World War. It is difficult in the light of events after 1904 to believe in imperialism as a prime motivating force in international affairs; and in the light of what we now know about the occupation of Egypt and its consequences for the flow of capital and revenue, it is difficult to see the European powers as engaged in enacting the last stages of capitalism.

It has been pointed out in the past how reluctant at least the British government was in its imperialising; and it is easy to point to the same characteristic in France.[8] In both cases it is striking how imperial feeling came to replace resentment at the financial cost of expansion only after expansion had already occurred. Under these circumstances the question of motive becomes less easy to answer; and explanations expressed in the language of the dialectic or of Rudyard Kipling appear irrelevant. Part of the answer is to be found in the fact that what brought the European powers into action was the collapse of native regimes. Developed western technological societies possessed totally different methods, preoccupations and expectations, and their effect on less developed areas was destructive, albeit unintentionally. Indeed, the last thing that western governments wanted was local collapse; but ironically everything that they did to shore up the existing regimes, contributed to their eventual disappearance, by further undermining the spiritual and practical bases of their existence. This development was by no means confined to Africa, or to North Africa. It had already occurred across India, and was beginning to be felt in central Asia as the Russians advanced eastwards. Before long it would destroy the ancient society of Persia and render that country an insoluble problem of Anglo-Russian relations, insoluble even under the umbrella of the 1907 convention.

Thus, as the later nineteenth century wore on, and the reach of European civilisation grew longer, the effects of this confrontation became more obvious. In their efforts to encourage, install and support native regimes, the powers merely discovered that so far from rendering themselves supernumerary, they were being sucked ever further into local politics. Assistance became military support against nationalist movements which had resented the assistance; military support finally rendered incompetent governments unacceptable; and the price of permanent support had to be an end to incompetence. So support slid into control, and control into colonial government.

But if it is possible to explain why the opportunity for expansion occurred as it did, this is not a sufficient explanation for the other half of the question: why did the European powers feel it necessary, however reluctantly, to take these opportunities? It would be possible to observe that governments behave in this way out of habit; that in a steady slide into occupation, each step seems to those who decide to take it an obvious and hardly significant action. It is equally possible to point to strategic considerations, and note that for Britain the routes to India were of unusual moment: in those areas Britain could not tolerate chaos. Again, in the case of France, it might be said rightly that it was difficult for the republican government to forbid advances made by the army in North Africa, even if it did not want desert for an empire, since the defeated officers of 1870 were more safely occupied in the rear of Algeria than they might be supporting generals such as Boulanger who wanted revenge against Germany in Europe.[9] Nor were Bismarck's constant promptings that France should compensate herself abroad for the lost provinces entirely ineffective.[10]

Yet there remains the feeling that not even a combination of these factors with the use that Bismarck made of them, quite explains the anxiety which the powers exhibited about the whole problem. This effectively prevented them from putting it on ice – which they would often have dearly liked to do. There was an interlocking in the 1880s of the local developments, just noted, with an increase of tension in Europe as a whole which helps to account for the negative character of much of this imperial activity. Often annexation took place in order to forestall another power, not for the sake of the territory concerned. Similarly there was a marked emphasis on strategic objectives. The way in which the powers reacted to formal imperialism in Africa was an indication of the way the wind was blowing, and an indication of what Bismarck was up against in his struggle to immobilise international politics in the interests of Berlin.

The position that Egypt held in the minds of the French was greatly complicated by history. The expedition to the Nile organised by the first Napoleon, and the enormous amount of French capital laid out in the Levant generally, made the eastern Mediterranean an area of French interest. The threat that Napoleon's campaign had vaguely suggested was subtly altered in its mode of expression, but was nevertheless repeated, when de Lesseps constructed the Suez Canal. It did not remain a French undertaking, but it did remain a French tradition. Yet, like all essays in formal expansion at this time, when the Khedive of Egypt's rule, like that of the Bey of Tunis, became intolerable the suggestion of action was most unpopular. Had Gambetta remained in power in France, joint action, which the British urged and he favoured, might have been arranged. But Freycinet, his successor as Prime Minister, would not do the same and eventually, despite invitations from London, unilateral occupation took place in September 1882. Moreover, it took place without the French and without the possibility that the French could insist that eventually the British withdraw. They had not wanted Egypt for themselves, but they did want either an Egypt free from foreign control or compensation for what foreign control now existed. The British under Mr Gladstone disliked the whole affair heartily. They genuinely and persistently asserted the temporary nature of their occupation and were disinclined to offer the French anything. When it became clear that they had to remain in Egypt for good, or at least for the foreseeable future, they were not moved to pay the French for leaving them in Egypt, when they could in no circumstances be thrown out. When they did settle with France, after twenty years of embitterment, it was not their bad conscience over the events of 1882 which spurred them on, but their joint anxiety about the behaviour of the German government.

Only in one particular were the effects of the occupation felt over purely Egyptian affairs. When the British occupied Egypt, they believed that they would soon be able to depart, because they still hoped that the Concert of Europe might be induced to work in a formal sense, and that they would be able to secure international control. They consequently retained the international financial commission whose duty was to guard the interests of the largely French bondholders. This meant that they could not use Egyptian revenues to improve the administration of Egypt, since they had already been pledged to the service of the loans, whose safety the commission was there to protect. Since the French, humiliated as they had been, were most unlikely to agree to any suggestion the British might make, it behoved the British to try to secure the co-operation of Germany, as it did the French, for their own opposite reasons. For Bismarck, this was an opportunity to exert influence over the British, and to try to bind the French to himself as tightly and for as long as possible.

It is likely that Bismarck had already contemplated Egypt as a point of Anglo-French discord, for he had urged the British to take it for some time – in fact since before the Congress of Berlin. By the mid-eighties, however, when French resentment was beginning to mount, he was presented with a crisis in the Near East which made the supporting of France quite essential if the Three Emperors' League was to survive intact. Bulgaria had thrown off Russian tutelage, and provoked St Petersburg to thoughts of intervention, with all that that implied for Russo-Austrian relations. To have Russia estranged from Austria, and France estranged from Britain suggested a possible joint solution to their separate problems which Bismarck must avoid at all costs.

Skilful use of the Egyptian question was not the only means that Germany employed to protect herself from the consequences of Austro-Russian conflict. As so much that Bismarck did was devoted to the construction or maintenance of the system surrounding the 1879 alliance, it is not surprising to see him in 1883 make the first serious concession to Austria, in the Balkans. Roumania was joined to the Triple Alliance, and though this extension in no way represented German encouragement for such aims as the Habsburgs might have – indeed, quite the reverse – it was nevertheless the first indication that in less careful hands Germany might find herself dragged by Austria into Balkan adventures.[11] Unable to risk alienating Vienna by calling a halt, she yet provoked calamity by her acquiescence. Nor was Bismarck's position made any more comfortable by the suggestion that the Three Emperors' League might not be renewed by Russia in 1883 on the same terms as hitherto. It was an unnecessary scare, but it was what Bismarck feared most and therefore what he was most ready to fear. It was all the more important to keep France in dependence on Germany, and that meant that she must quarrel with Britain and find support at Berlin and nowhere else. The quarrel with Britain was happily arranged in Egypt; all that Bismarck had to do was to keep the fires burning long enough to achieve his ends.

The French, spurred into West-African activity by their recent humiliation, reacted vigorously to the establishment of Leopold of Belgium's private colony on the Congo, and sent their own great explorer, de Brazza, to claim the north bank of the river. The British were moved as ever by the feeling that no owner at all would be the better solution; but that, if owner there had to be, they preferred the least protectionist state. They therefore arranged a somewhat shady deal which made use of an ancient and defunct Portuguese claim to the whole area. The French were understandably displeased, and Bismarck began operations on his own account.

He proposed a revival of the old league of armed neutrality, formed against Britain during the American War, and caused his consul at Cape Town to announce that a concession in South West Africa was under German protection. The negotiations that followed this were muddled. They were such as to convince one historian that what Bismarck was trying to do was not so much found a German colonial empire as make the British understand what sort of a power Germany had become, and adjust her conduct accordingly.[12] The British, by their complete misunderstanding of what was afoot, forced Bismarck into actual occupation, which he did not intend. This is attractive, because it explains the extraordinary fashion in which the British, who evidently did not care about South West Africa, and in any case preferred the lower German tariffs to the French, were pursued by Bismarck relentlessly beyond any point at which he might have been expected to be satisfied. But all this was certainly for more profound a purpose than to make the British sit up and take notice; it was largely for the sake of the new Franco-German *entente*. Nevertheless, the British, incompetently guided by Lord Granville (briefly Foreign Secretary), revealed that they did not yet understand the new spirit of expansionism that was abroad and still thought that colonies were temporary misfortunes wished upon powers, rather than the other way about. They retreated continuously, and did not need to be in receipt of a famous despatch which Bismarck never sent warning them against opposing German imperialism – though he characteristically banked it against a future quarrel with Britain. South West Africa was chosen, as was New Guinea in the following year, for the effect it might have on neighbouring British colonists. It was readily ceded, despite the colonists' revealing statement that they did not mind having Germans as neighbours, but that they preferred to have no neighbours at all.[13] Meanwhile a new conference on the Egyptian bondholders threatened to produce an unsafe degree of Anglo-French discord, and it was allowed to break up without result. Thereupon Bismarck produced further anti-British devices, like the conservative gathering of the eastern emperors at Skierniwice in Poland, and further suggestions for the construction of a maritime league. This was not such an improbable suggestion as it sounded and was meant to be. The British rested contentedly on their naval superiority, but it was as tenuous a lead as at any point in the nineteenth century, and Britain could have been seriously embarrassed if any opposing maritime alliance had come about. So much so that a naval resurgence followed from the scare that she had endured in 1884.

What eventually emerged from Franco-German cooperation against Britain was not a league but a new conference at Berlin to settle the affairs of the Congo Basin. Again, sadly for Bismarck, it proved to be extremely difficult to maintain the anti-British front. Indeed, it soon appeared that what Britain wanted was closer to German desires than anything else, and she was perfectly content with the result of the conference. Her arrangement with Portugal had been, like everything else, a negative, preservative gesture and represented no positive desire of her own. When the conference recognised King Leopold's Association as neutral, her desire for low tariffs and equal competition was satisfied.

The nature of the German position in Europe was such, however, as will be seen, over and beyond the question of extending the area of the Concert of Europe, that the quarrel must continue. Bismarck arranged a dispute over the partition of New Guinea, which dragged on satisfactorily for months and quite upset the Australians, for whose appetite the government in London acquired an amazed respect. Meanwhile in Paris Jules Ferry, the French Prime Minister, was about to meet his Waterloo. The Franco-German *entente* had always depended to some extent on the interest which his government displayed in colonial affairs, as it had depended upon the willingness of Ferry himself to be realistic about the possibilities of regaining Alsace-Lorraine. He could swallow and resist the anti-German prejudice that was so deeply seated in France, and temporarily co-operate with Germany. Other French governments would more likely reveal the true opinions of the majority of Frenchmen, and resist the blandishments of Bismarck, while opposing colonial adventures. Courcel, the French ambassador in Berlin, and Ferry were never undiscriminating in their co-operation with Bismarck, and warily avoided the binding *entente*, which the Chancellor would have liked to create. It is significant that when later French governments rejected the imperial legacy of Ferry, Bismarck dropped colonialism as a means of bringing about goodwill in France and instant quarrels with Britain.

A small defeat in Indo-China, which Ferry was in the process of wresting from the Chinese for France, brought him down by causing a combination of the disparate elements which had always been suspicious of his politics. His departure was the beginning of the end of Franco-German co-operation. However, the Russians induced a new situation for a short time by threatening Afghanistan from the north. They had been advancing steadily for some time, and the British government had been in some anxiety as to whether the dreaded question of Russian designs upon India would not soon be raised. The Penjdeh dispute –about an area on the northern frontier of Afghanistan – brought it perilously near, for the Russians now established themselves round Merv, and there was no way in which the British could bring pressure to bear. The Russians were not genuinely trying to threaten the British position in India, but they were very anxious to make the British think that they were. Giers, the Russian Foreign Minister, said that he wanted a 'defensive position against the hostility displayed by the British government towards us since the Crimean war'.[14] The consequence was that the British thought seriously of attacking the Russians through the Straits; and against this danger the European powers acted with united disapproval. The result was a compelling demonstration of continental solidarity against Britain, and the closest Bismarck ever came to success in organising a continental league. It was also the end of such a possibility.[15] For once the Russians were assured that the Straits were safe, they had no need of their 'defensive position' and could compromise with Britain in the Penjdeh dispute. The French were no longer prepared to back Germany in colonial disputes with Britain, as was shown by Freycinet's reluctance to follow Bismarck in a dispute in East Africa. This was as well, because in East Africa there was for Britain a strategic need to defend her position on the Nile; and Salisbury was ready to expand for that purpose, as eventually he did. But Freycinet was warned by Ferry's example, and was soon in any case tied by a newly nationalist Chamber, elected in 1885. Also in 1885, the somewhat confused government of Mr Gladstone was replaced, and Lord Salisbury returned to the Foreign Office. Salisbury, though he could not have prevented the period of illwill between Germany and Britain, was at least more perceptive than Granville, and would not have been such an uncomprehending assistance to Bismarck. Now he expressed his desire to co-operate with Germany, and found a Bismarck, claiming to be disillusioned by the French but in reality successful in his objectives, who was quite willing to change his tune.

The whole colonial episode of 1884–5 left a very unpleasant taste in the British mouth, and the violence of some of Bismarck's language, directed for the first time against Britain, did nothing to erase the sense of puzzled resentment at what appeared to be a gratuitous campaign to discomfort Britain all over the world. It was, of course, a long time since Britain had been forced into dependence upon her continental colleagues for the conduct of her policies, and it was least partially Lord Granville's failure to recognise that this had indeed become the case, which sharpened the course of international politics during these years. That the affair had a continuing importance is shown by the way in which, when international affairs later took on a different and more menacing aspect, Bismarck's behaviour was frequently referred to, both within and without the British Foreign Office, as marking the beginning of a decline in the tone and conduct of Anglo-German relations.[16] In fact, some of this was unjustified. It was only after the British came to value their imperial domination and prospects that they minded what appeared to have been an attack upon them. Before this, they seemed unable to grasp what the fuss was about. They also exaggerated the significance of the unsent warning, when they came to hear of it via a subsequent reference the Chancellor made to it in the *Reichstag*. But there was no doubt that new preoccupations and some new methods had entered the political arena, and that they had done so for the reasons noted.

Internal German politics, however, also had a part to play. Historians have observed the paradox in Bismarck's reiterations of the importance of the purely European map in considering German security; his vigorous denunciations of the case put forward by the German colonial lobby, and his annexations of 1884–5.[17] They have therefore searched for something more immediately compelling than the safety of his international arrangements to account for his sudden conversion to the principle of colonial annexations. Such people have tended to accept the argument that his son Herbert Bismarck, the Foreign Secretary, repeated in 1890: 'When we started colonial policy, we had to face a long reign by the Crown Prince during which English influence would predominate. In order to forestall this, we had to launch colonial policy which is popular, and can produce conflicts with England at any moment. '[18] This argument was used by Bismarck the elder on several occasions to justify rushing legislation he wanted, or in preparing measures against a possible anti-autocratic bias in the government. He does not seem to have believed seriously in the risk of anglicisation or liberalisation, however, nor did he complain of the Emperor Frederick during his short reign.

What is much more characteristic and more to the point was his attitude to the *Reichstag*. He was, of course, delighted to humiliate the Liberal government of Mr Gladstone, and thus read a lesson to German admirers of genuine parliamentary democracy, but he was even more concerned to improve the management of such parliamentary democracy as he was unhappily committed to already. For he was enduring the worst period of his relationship with the *Reichstag*, and elections were approaching. He was already using the danger from socialists as a weapon to secure obedience, and he was deprived of his usual source of foreign scares as the Germans could not on this occasion be threatened with danger from France, as in 1875, or from Russia. Britain might rise to the colonial bait, and thus please the growing body of opinion which was demanding colonial expansion – for the same sort of economic–patriotic reasons as Jules Ferry was urging it on the French – as well as generating sufficient enthusiasm to secure a favourable result at the elections. These pressures, though stronger in a country which did not have overseas possessions or the experience of them were additionally motivated by the general belief that colonies brought power and authority instead of being their consequence. But they were not so strong that Bismarck had to give way to public demands. He claimed that he was doing just that, but when he wished to stop, he stopped, and nothing that the Colonial League could say affected his decision. He gave to Germany a scrappy empire, and the desire for more; he also bequeathed to her the general view that she could not get more because of the implacable opposition of Britain. Both were sad inheritances, but not so sad as the expectation that a manufactured foreign crisis could be successfully used to spike socialist guns, cajole the *Reichstag* or browbeat a future emperor. Bismarck's primary aim was none of these things, they were secondary: he desired to protect his web surrounding Germany, shielding her from the consequences of unification, and he was successful.

In the longer term, however, it was clear that the whole episode had enlarged the scope of the Concert of Europe, as it had not been enlarged since the end of the Crimean War, even if on this occasion the reason lay less obviously within the area absorbed and more in the growing problems of Germany. It is also interesting to observe how the expansion had proved to be controllable, but that this control could not be expressed in the familiar tone of Concert diplomacy.

III

The next occasion on which the Concert of Europe confronted the non-European world was of far greater significance, and occurred exactly ten years later.

The reach of European civilisation, particularly with the aid of the electric telegraph and the steamship, let alone its economic energy, began to be formidably apparent even in the more distant areas towards the end of the nineteenth century. The result was a change in the nature of international power in which its expression became more and more technological, and caused an upset in traditional relationships both between powers and between different parts of the world. This change in the currency of international power coupled with the emergence beyond Europe of new powers, dealing also in the new currency, faced the great powers with a world-wide sphere of international operation in which the old bases of the international system in Europe had become geographically and practically inappropriate. Like the new preoccupations of European governments, this development had a sapping effect on the European Concert, and rendered it too weak to withstand the effects of a new internal disparity caused by the predominance of Germany.

Events in the Far East between 1895 and 1905 provide fascinating examples of the damaging effect which followed when European states were forced to operate on a world-wide basis. The situation there produced a most unfortunate interaction whereby local problems tended to become European problems (because the presence of the powers inevitably carried them back to the home foreign offices) and the tensions within Europe were added to those already existing: both fed upon each other and were magnified. Of course it was true that, particularly in the case of Austro-Russian conflict, European problems were, over a very short time-scale, in some ways eased by Russia's involvement in the Far East. But when deadlock in the Far East again concentrated European problems in Europe, the weakening effect of Far-Eastern conflicts made it much harder for the Concert to withstand the consequent strain.

The root difficulty was that the Far East already contained an international system in embryo. The absence of the United States from the European scene did not signify her total isolation from all international politics, and with the annexation of the Philippines Guam and Hawaii in 1898, the United States completed her advance across the Pacific by becoming a Far-Eastern power. Russia, too, had been present on the Amur river for some decades but, with the near completion of the Trans-Siberian Railway in 1895, she became a potentially major force, and the first great power to be able to exert pressure in the Far East without having to reckon with British sea-power. Japan, from the Meiji restoration in 1867, rapidly advanced until after the Sino-Japanese War of 1895 and, indisputably after the war with Russia of 1903–5, she was recognised as a great power. From the point of view of the future, the confrontation which began to emerge between the United States and Russia was of profound significance, and soon changed traditionally good relations into perennially bad ones.[19] The same development that was weakening the European Concert was destined in the end to eclipse it altogether. The conduct of international politics on a world stage soon brought out the antagonisms of the two genuine world powers; a cloud no bigger than a man's hand as yet, but the first indications of a storm beside which the preparing catastrophe in Europe would seem to be only a beginning. Nevertheless, the European catastrophe was brought appreciably nearer by the consequences of this meeting between the Concert and newer forces which it could not control.

The second difficulty in the Far East was very similar to the problem of the Ottoman Empire. The Manchu dynasty in China was collapsing, and ceasing to be able to extend its control far beyond the capital, Peking. The openings appeared to be there for the infiltration of western influence in commerce, religion and politics. The building of railways, the financing of loans, the extortion of concessions: all appeared to presage the partition of China.

The first unmistakable sign of the involvement of Europe with the Far East, as distinct from vague reactions to distant happenings, was the Triple Intervention of 1895, following the Sino-Japanese War. The gap between Japan and China had widened consistently as the effect of Japan's westernisation was felt. By 1895, she was ready to assert her domination by war, and quickly defeated China by both land and sea. She then compelled China to accept a Japanese puppet state in Korea, which was necessary for Japanese security, and, among other privileges, to cede the Liaotung peninsula, with Port Arthur. It was this last that provoked the Triple intervention of Russia, France and Germany. The Russians had just pushed the Trans-Siberian Railway through and had no intention of allowing Japan to seize their inheritance in China at the last moment. If the Japanese were allowed to retain their gains from the Treaty of Shimonoseki, they would be in a position to dominate Manchuria and, above all, Peking. To insist that Japan drop this condition of the peace, Russia persuaded both Germany and France to join in a protest at Tokyo. The reasons in both cases were wholly European. For Germany, the involvement of Russia in China was an opportunity to seek relief from pressure on the eastern frontier, and to distract her from the Balkans. For France, it was an opportunity to show Russia that her friendship was worth having because, for the sake of French security, Russian support must be retained. For precisely opposite reasons to those of Germany, France disliked Russian involvement in China, but so long as it was so, she had to make herself as useful as possible. There was, however, at least one reason why France and Germany could combine to support Russia in the Far East and agree upon their motives, and that was the chance to revive some sort of league against Britain. Together they could and did force Britain to permit reciprocal concessions in China. But the consequences of discomfiting Britain were in the end to have European results which only harmed the flexibility of the international system.

The battle for concessions followed the revision of the Treaty of Shimonoseki, as the Russians brought their now preponderant force to bear upon the Chinese. Loans, railways, extra-territorial rights along the railway lines: all were forced upon the Chinese, with French assistance and thus consequent French concessions in Tongking. German assistance and German gains also followed, unwanted though they were by the Russo-French combination. For Germany was placed in an awkward position. On the one hand, the demands of common sense dictated that she should support Russia, for the sake of peace and quiet in Vienna; and on the other, the dictates of *Weltpolitik* – now in the hands of Bülow – urged a policy of independent annexations in opposition to Russia. By 1897, Germany was only capable of deciding to pursue both policies at once, and in that year she seized Kiaochow on the Shantung Peninsula. The excuse was, significantly, the murder of two Roman Catholic German missionaries, which raised unusual support in the *Reichstag* from the Catholic Centre. This seizure produced a disagreeable effect in international politics, and was quickly followed by reciprocal demands. Russia secured Port Arthur, France obtained the lease of Kwangchowwan, between Indo-China and Hong Kong, and Britain forced the Chinese to concede Weihaiwei, also on the Shantung coast. A contest then arose in the allotting of spheres of influence, and the tone of communications between the powers and China, and between themselves, was reduced to the level of ultimatums. During 1898, there was a serious risk that Chinese disputes might cause the outbreak of a European war.

The situation was eased, however, by the maturing of the Fashoda crisis (see chapter 5, section III). This had the double effect of weakening French support for Russia, who showed herself singularly unmoved by France's African troubles, and convincing her that British sea-power made the prospect of an Anglo-Russian war singularly uninviting, let alone an Anglo-French conflict. The Fashoda crisis failed to extort compensation from Britain for the occupation of Egypt, as had all previous French *démarches*, and the lesson finally learnt drew France along the path towards the *Entente* of 1904.[20] Furthermore, the seizure of the Philippines by the United States in 1898 served to give Britain a much needed ally. For Germany had sought to make what she could out of the Spanish-American War of that year, and attempted to prevent the American capture of Manila. The weaker American fleet was successful only through the timely aid of a British squadron, and subsequent American possession of the Philippines was a much safer proposition, at least to begin with, provided that Washington retained the goodwill of Britain. The Americans, who had no interest in acquiring territory in China, and possessed none, were able to adopt the policy that Britain had been forced to abandon: they insisted upon the 'open door'. In 1899 Britain was able to enjoy the satisfaction of seeing her preferred policy embodied in the circular issued by the Secretary of State, John Hay. It was, Professor Barraclough has written, 'noteworthy as the first occasion on which the United States made a pronouncement of a general character concerning affairs outside the American continent'.[21] Only Russia refused to accept it.

The result was a welcome relaxation of tension, followed in 1900 by the need for a combined reaction to the Boxer Rising. This was a last kick by the expiring body of traditionalist China, and its sole permanent result was the occupation of Manchuria by Russia. This in turn convinced the British that the time had come when they must seek an ally. Russian advances in the Far East had for some time provoked discussions about an alliance, and the effect of the isolated unpopularity which the Boer War had brought merely added point to the argument. For assistance in the Far East the only possible allies were Germany and Japan. Germany was sounded for an agreement repeatedly between 1898 and 1901, but no arrangement was forthcoming. A brief co-operation against Russia was entered into in 1901, specifically in China, but no sooner was the agreement in force, than Bülow informed the *Reichstag* that it did not apply to Manchuria, which was the one place where Britain wanted it to have effect. This may have been the end of Britain's desire for an agreement with Germany; it was certainly the beginning of serious thought of an agreement with Japan – possibly with Germany as a third party. The Japanese were wary. They had always wanted an agreement with Russia, believing that they and the Russians alone were fundamentally interested in China. But the Russians would not compromise their ambitions until they had been defeated in war, and constant Japanese approaches met with rebuffs. If, on the other hand, the Japanese were going to be forced to fight the Russians, then certainly they needed an ally, and only Britain was suitable. After the Russians had again refused a Japanese offer, the Anglo-Japanese Alliance was signed on 30 January 1902.[22]

This alliance was not only significant for being the first serious agreement made by any European power with an Asiatic state, nor even because it was the Asiatic party which gained the most but also because it had a European consequence of immense importance. The alternative to an agreement with Russia on the part of Japan was war. Only hindsight could give to Japan in such a war the certain victory which eventually resulted. She believed, and the other powers believed, that the assistance of Britain would be required. Such expectations led the Kaiser to remark of the British when the alliance was made: 'the noodles have had a lucid interval'.[23] He had been recommending an Anglo-Japanese agreement for years in the belief that such an alignment would embroil Britain further with Russia. Anglo-Russian conflict the Germans had come to regard as preordained, but they were always anxious to twist the knife if the opportunity arose. The situation, however, would look very different if British estimates of Japanese military potential were correct and the Russians were defeated easily. Such a defeat could only follow in any case from the existence of an Anglo-Japanese alliance, even if the physical assistance of Britain was not required; for without it the Japanese would not risk a conflict. Such a defeat could also only have the effect of turning Russia back from China towards the Balkans, with all that implied for Austro-Russian relations. Nor were the Germans wise to rejoice and ignore the effect of the alliance upon France. Conflict between her and Britain had also seemed in Berlin to be permanent. But if the French had decided that Fashoda meant that they must avoid conflicts with Britain, the Anglo-Japanese Alliance faced them with the need either to abandon their agreement with Russia, which they could not do, or to find the means to be able to prevent Britain from assisting Japan actively in the coming war with Russia. The immediate result of the alliance was a Franco-Russian declaration of protection for China, but the real consequence was the Anglo-French *Entente* of 1904.

The Russo-Japanese War duly took place, and the Japanese were wholly victorious both by land and sea. Various alarms and excursions accompanied the conflict, particularly the Dogger Bank incident, in which the Russian Baltic fleet, sailing to Japanese waters, supposed itself to have encountered Japanese vessels, when in fact it had fired on British fishermen off the Dogger Bank. The sharp exchanges that followed were just contained peacefully. More seriously perhaps, the Germans, after making much of their assistance to the Russian fleet, in fact failed to supply it with coal beyond the coast of Africa, and their attempts to make capital out of the Dogger Bank incident by proposing again a German–French–Russian combination against Britain failed to do more than irritate all parties. For Germany the policy of the free hand was fast becoming the possession of an empty hand. The hostility of Russia and France towards Britain was waning, largely as a result of the war in the Far East: it would not be long before having an empty hand led to accusations of encirclement from Berlin.

The 1905 Treaty of Portsmouth (New Hampshire) which ended the Russo-Japanese War was concluded in the United States, after American mediation, and it effectively brought the Far-Eastern crisis to an end, at least before 1914. There was no doubt at all that the Far-Eastern crisis had not been solved by the Concert of Europe. The European great powers had not succeeded in making the move from being active and frequently angry participants in the scramble for China to being the kind of demarcating, controlling agents that had emerged from the Berlin conference on Africa; still less had they achieved the utter certainty of the Peace of Paris of 1856.

In more detailed terms there is no doubt that the whole episode greatly soured relationships between some European powers. In particular, powers had been shocked by the violence of Germany's reaction in seizing Kiaochow. But perhaps most important of all was the clarifying effect that events in China had upon Anglo-German relations and, indeed, upon the basic stance of the British Empire.

There was always a major and decisive difficulty about attempting to introduce a formal and positive improvement into Anglo-German relations, which were becoming poorer, but for reasons which were difficult to explain, because to do so required a recognition of the world base upon which international relations now rested. Germany wished to be a world power because she recognised the latent threat from Russia – a threat which existed in Europe. The British, however, until 1907, desired to improve their position in relation to Russia outside Europe, and particularly in the Far East. A British desire for German assistance against Russia outside Europe could not meet and make a successful agreement with Germany's desire for British support against Russia – and by extension France – inside Europe. This is shown with complete clarity by the otherwise incomprehensible failure of the Anglo-German Yangtse Basin Agreement of 1900.

The other side of this coin can be seen in the stepping-up of attempts by the British government to obtain a supporting agreement for use in the Far East – a process which was to lead the British Empire out of isolation. Salisbury first tried to get an agreement with Russia, on the basis of making a straightforward compromise with his principal opponent. Interestingly the Russians now believed that there was no need for such a compromise – at last they were genuinely untouchable and free agents in the Far East, as they had always tried to be in the Near East. And it is fascinating to watch the geographical stretch of the proposed compromise: the British actually got as far as hinting that they would be willing to see an alteration in the status of Constantinople in exchange for a Chinese agreement. This proposal was revolutionary in the European context, but at this point profoundly uninteresting to the Russians, who did not think that they needed to exchange a European gain for a Far-Eastern loss. This would not have been conceivable after 1856 or again after 1905. The British government then embarked on the first of many attempts to gain an anti-Russian agreement with the Germans, all of which were destined to fail, and eventually in January 1902 made an alliance with Japan. This was possible because with the Japanese the regional logic worked. The British wanted a stable position for themselves, particularly *vis-à-vis* the Russians, and the Japanese thought they needed an ally in the event of a Russo-Japanese war: the basis was wholly local. But once again the interlocked nature of international affairs affecting the Far East began to show. The 1902 alliance was not the only cause of the Anglo-French *Entente*, but it was a very important one. With that agreement, Britain's emergence into European affairs was begun, and its first consequence was a major European crisis, leading to the Algeçiras conference of 1906.

The Far-Eastern crisis, however, did not just have the effect of embroiling Anglo-German relations: it also had the effect of improving

Austro-Russian and therefore Russo-German relations. If the Near East was exchanged for the Far East as the area of Russian interference and advance, the traditional difficulty in Austro-Russian relations was removed and with it the traditional restraint upon Germany, brought about by her anxiety not to allow a Near-Eastern crisis to lead to an uncontrollable German-Russian quarrel. The licentiousness of German policy between 1896 and 1905 and her constant assertions that she had a free hand owe something to this happy bonus. But nothing that Germany did while enjoying this favourable situation contributed to her own security, indeed quite the reverse, and when the realities of the European situation reverted to normal after 1905, they did so in circumstances where the whole structure of international relations had been changed for the worse. This is why the tone of relations between the powers became so rapidly alarming when, after 1905, the centre of gravity in international politics returned to Europe. Thus it may be seen how, in the history of the collapse of the Concert of Europe, its failure to extend the accepted area of operation to the Far East was a highly significant development.

Further Reading

G. Barraclough, *An Introduction to Contemporary History* (Pelican, 1967).

G. F. Hudson, *The Far East in World Politics* (Oxford: OUP, 1937).

W. L. Langer, *European Alliances and Alignments, 1870–1890* (Knopf, 1950).

——, *The Diplomacy of Imperialism, 1890–1902* (Knopf, 1951).

R. E. Robinson and J. Gallagher with Alice Denny, *Africa and the Victorians* (Macmillan, 1963).

A. J. P. Taylor, *The Struggle for Mastery in Europe, 1848–1918* (Oxford: OUP, 1957).

A. P. Thornton, *Doctrines of Imperialism* (Wiley, 1965).

3. Inside Europe: Domestic Pressures and the Redistribution of Power in Central Europe

I

In any state, there is always a degree of interconnection between foreign and domestic policies. Sometimes, this is perfectly obvious, as in the case of the economic consequences of defence policies pursued in response to an overriding foreign threat. Sometimes it is commented upon, but is less obvious or quantifiable, as in the case of those German attitudes to British foreign policy – particularly in respect of her willingness to go to war – which were affected by the prolonged crisis in Ireland before 1914. In the event, there was no connection, but some outsiders – and a few insiders – thought that there might be. Naturally the detail and atmosphere of all states' policies were affected by internal considerations. But only in the case of Germany and Austria was the fundamental stance of their policy heavily influenced by fears for the safety of their regimes. For them, either the possession of very great power, as in the case of Germany, or the absolute necessities dictated by an anachronistic state structure, as in the case of Austria, came to suggest the use of foreign policy as a weapon in domestic policy. Other states might have wished to do this: Russia perhaps after 1905, but she was prevented, or dared not, for lack of power. Italy also showed a similar tendency, but failed to make any serious impact, partly because of insufficient management, but principally because she operated only on a small scale. The interconnection is of more profound importance in the cases of Austria and Germany, not only because they each bred it naturally and strongly, but also because Germany – with serious consequences for her ally – was becoming the most powerful state in the world, thus producing a major change in the distribution of power. So for her it was the opportunity presented by the state of international affairs coupled with her own domestic situation that provided the mainspring of her policy. For the others, foreign policy became principally a reaction to the activities of the Triple Alliance. The response of Russia to the Bosnia

29

crisis of 1908–9, and of France to both the Morocco crises showed this (see chapter 6). In Britain, the same effect may be seen in the mutually incompatible responses which wanted both a naval extension at least the equal of Germany's, and sought to make determined efforts to achieve a *détente* with Germany, if necessary by appeasement. A fundamentally defensive stance came to characterise foreign policies of the other powers, and such an attitude was induced far more by external factors – the state of international politics and the policy of the Triple Alliance – than by any internal considerations. For them, the international system provided anxieties and uncertainties. It did so too for Germany; but for Germany alone did it provide opportunities. Thus the reason for Germany's domestic discomfort, and the springs of her power, have to be examined in some detail.

The problem in the case of Germany was initially constitutional.[1] The constitution of the North German Confederation had been in part a trade treaty, and in part a political arrangement, involving the creation of some legislative organs. It was a curious and in many ways unsatisfactory compilation, but the Confederation was run on the principle of Prussian domination, and that domination was protected by past annexations rather than by the constitution. There was no particular difficulty in knowing what was the distribution of political power; nor was Prussian society or the agrarian interest seriously threatened. The same could not be said of the situation which followed from the unification of 1871. The 'constitution' remained the same, though being now signed by the south German states, but the distribution of power and the protected position of Prussia were changed. The change was not greatly obvious until economic and then social developments – stemming principally from the onset of the German industrial revolution – created a danger to Prussian economic interests, even to Prussian society itself. The Second Reich had not come about in order to elevate the bourgeoisie of the south and west, or to preside over the creation of a heavy industrial mecca in the valley of the Ruhr: it was there, at least in Bismarck's mind, to underpin the security of Prussia.

Unfortunately the constitutional basis of 1871 entrenched neither the position of Prussia with complete certainty, nor any alternative wholly federal system; nor was the ultimate source of authority clear, and clearly subject to effective checks. In these circumstances, particularly after 1879, Bismarck began to employ the ambiguities in the constitution to repair its deficiencies in the matter of Prussian security.

The Chancellor employed three main weapons. First, he saw to it that the administrative structure of the Reich as it came to be developed was largely inherited from Prussia, and that its personnel were almost exclusively drawn from the Prussian upper class. The first was achieved readily enough, since the constitution did not envisage a central Reich administration beyond the states' meeting of representatives – the *Bundesrat* – the Emperor and the Chancellor. The Chancellor himself was dependent on the *Reichstag* for authority in some matters, but dependent on the Emperor for his office: thus was the basis of authority obscured. Bismarck's response was not in the least obscure. All Reich administrative offices were held to be offshoots of the Chancellor's office, and the heads of such offices were officials and in no sense ministers subject to the scrutiny of the *Reichstag*. As their numbers increased there was little sign of any development into a Cabinet as it might be understood in other countries; and every effort made by the liberal parties in the *Reichstag* to instil the doctrine of ministerial responsibility was, and was doomed to be, a failure. One of the consequences of the slow development of genuine Reich institutions was the use of the Prussian government, conveniently present in Berlin, to fill in the gaps. The two systems became closely intertwined, so that when Bismarck's successor, Caprivi, tried to separate the imperial and Prussian functions of the chancellor and Minister-President, the governmental machine broke down. The practice of Prussian control of the organs of government was made secure by Bismarck through his comprehension of the immense power which control over economic policy was beginning to confer. The circumstances of the change to protection in 1879 showed how it was possible for the Chancellor to proffer economic gains to particular groups outside the political process and thereby tie them to the existing governmental system.[2] The fact of Prussian control was in effect exchanged for the possibility of variation from strictly Prussian economic interests. The result was a further diffusion of power, and further room for manoeuvre by those who wished to maintain the interests of Prussia against the interests of the Reich as a whole. The consequence of this was not at first unsettling: in the hands of Bismarck, any system that did something to overcome the confusion inherent in the political arrangements of the Reich was probably helpful, so long as there was no lapse of authority itself. When that happened, as it did, there was to be no alternative to expedient shifts of policy and the passing influence of different coteries.

The second weapon that the Chancellor employed was that of the partial solution. The new industrial revolution produced, as might have been expected, uncomfortable social and political strains. As far as Bismarck was concerned, it most particularly signalled the advance to significant political power of the Social Democratic Party (SPD), a development which was as alarming as any that could occur to a devoted Prussian nationalist. His method was to put the SPD under serious political disadvantages through discriminatory legislation, but to try to achieve important parts of their programme himself, thus to some extent drawing their teeth. In this way the chance of reforming the machinery of government was reduced, and the protection of Prussia assured; by this means also was the practice of appeasement rather than cure elevated almost to a principle of government – whether by Bismarck or Bülow.

Thirdly, the Chancellor used the weapon of foreign crises in order to ease the insoluble problem posed by the divided basis of power. Since the *Reichstag* could neither appoint nor dismiss the Chancellor or members of his Cabinet, there was always the possibility of a conflict between the government and a majority in Parliament – yet over some matters of finance, particularly grants for the army, the consent of the *Reichstag* had to be obtained. Therefore the Chancellor, in order to satisfy the Emperor to whom he owed his appointment, had to be able to organise a majority over such matters. Bismarck's favourite device in this situation was to arrange a foreign crisis, sometimes accompanied by a war-scare. For reasons discussed in chapter 5, it was safe for Bismarck to use the international situation in this way: but it would not always be so, and it was to be highly dangerous that the notion had become an accepted part of German political behaviour.

Bismarck was largely successful during his time as Chancellor, but his success was principally due to the understanding that he enjoyed with William I. This convergence of mind, or in some cases the Emperor's willingness to concede, meant that there was no confusion of authority at the centre while the partnership lasted. It can easily be realised, however, that the peculiar situation of the Chancellor rendered him extremely vulnerable to an Emperor who wished to govern by himself – or even indulged in the passing whim – since it was always possible for the Emperor to be his own Chancellor and appoint a man of straw to the formal post. But the result, if the Emperor's direction was uncertain in any way, would be the general decline of central control, since the Chancellor's authority would be reduced, and the Emperor's remain doubtful. With the accession of William II, just such a situation arose.

Even if the Kaiser's importance was not so great as historians, perhaps impressed by the desire of the allies to hang him in 1919, have in the past suggested, he is nevertheless a fascinating and important figure. The first fact to be clear about, if it was not known before, is that he had a withered arm. Pictures of him were taken so that this disability was not obvious. His tutors – and indeed his grandmother, Queen Victoria, who complained about him from Windsor continuously – reported that he had no application and could not work. He thought that they were dunderheads. Curiously, they were both right. William had a light-weight intellect, which was nevertheless capable of sudden striking understandings and appreciations. His tutors disapproved too strongly of lack of concentration to notice the odd brilliant patch. His intellect was too small to appreciate what could not be truly understood without the acquisition of knowledge. He was like his grandmother in that he had a sense – nowhere near as well-developed as hers – of what the bourgeoisie were feeling. He would have hated to be thought so, but he was a typical middle-class German of his period. Although he came from the highest social stratum, he was deprived of the sense of assurance which frequently goes with such a position, by virtue of the inferiority complex which sprang from the withered arm. Either this or other physiological causes brought on depressions and nervous disorder generally, particularly at moments of crisis. As a result he was unbalanced, and it was just at moments of crisis that his judgement could not be trusted. But where the modern historian differs from the contemporary observer is in knowing that it was just at moments of crisis that his judgement was ignored. Despite the bluster, despite the high-flown claims, William in fact gave way over every major difference of opinion with his advisers. It took time and energy to wear him down and the result was always a nervous collapse, but it is tragically the case that at the very moment when by his exaggerated claims and appalling behaviour he was devaluing the Chancellorship, he was unable to replace it with a steady authority of his own. It was not true that William was not fit to rule. He had the gift of rapidly sizing up complex problems, and he had the determination to rule to a quite alarming extent. Quite possibly in any other country, his obvious mental instability and frequently paranoid public utterances would have led at least to the application of some restraints. In Germany, his speeches were widely regarded as disastrous, but they were not so far from probability as to be regarded as mad, and his devoted coterie of courtiers took all possible steps to conceal his lapses. William's own charm and confidential manner served to make it impossible for government ministers to convince those not in the know of the true situation. There was always therefore a time-lag during which William could safely dispose of the disillusioned and begin again with those successfully enticed by flattery. Thus what looked like an inevitable and healthy show-down was postponed *sine die*, or until it was absorbed into the apotheosis of war.[3]

He had always to be more of the prevailing majority opinion than anyone else, otherwise he would not feel safe: thus he was always more German, more Prussian, more landowning, more expansionist, and – perhaps his one real opinion – more naval than everyone else. This attitude chimed in well with the attitude of imitation adopted by the middle class for the old Prussian aristocracy. It is well illustrated by his feelings towards Britain. He never forgot that he was half British, or that his grandmother had died in his arms – that does seem to have been the one state occasion when William behaved really well, they were usually too much for his nerves – and took mostly a great pride in his other nationality. He used to send the British Admiralty useful hints on how to run a navy, even at moments of the most extreme hostility, and he always claimed that he had told the War Office how to win the Boer War and that his advice had been taken. But he was also jealous. When he was in Britain the power, the state pageantry, the unified kingdom, the long-settled tradition made him feel an admiring pride; when he got home again, he tended to feel inferior and to relapse into suspicions that Edward VII was encircling him as a deliberate policy, or that he was being ignored, and to react by becoming violently pro-German, uttering terse warnings, very reminiscent of the schoolboy threatening teacher with his mother. And yet with all this he did not take the final decisions. The men who did had to have his confidence, but they could make him do what they wanted. And they were not politicians, nor even always soldiers or sailors; they were quite often simply cronies. Michael Balfour says of William II:

> He contributed materially by his example and influence to that false assessment of values and to that unsoundness of judgement which . . . was Germany's basic weakness. He was a distracting rather than a steadying influence, who, instead of helping his ministers to identify and pursue the ends which really mattered, impeded the cool objective study of Germany's problems. Holding a position in which he could have done much to counteract the tendencies around him he instead gave them added emphasis.[4]

In Bismarck's immediate successor, changes were naturally least evident. It was as little true of home affairs as it was of foreign that Bismarck was too great a man to be succeeded, or that his policies were too difficult to be repeated. It was simply that circumstances changed so that the adoption of sensible policies became extremely difficult and not surprisingly new Chancellors failed. It was not so much that the quality of Chancellors declined, as that the importance of the office was diminished. General Leo von Caprivi succeeded as Chancellor and Minister-President of Prussia in 1890. He was no man's fool and unlikely to be any man's puppet. His independent simplicity made him at times surprisingly naïve, but his policy was to be one of reconciliation. Bismarck had gone out amidst a hail of typical abuse, the worse for the magnificent earthiness which he always employed, and Caprivi claimed that although he would now pursue the same general lines, he would reconcile those whom Bismarck's readiness to offend had unnecessarily alienated. Abroad, the government would abandon ambiguity and complexity and adopt a simple policy of the protection of German interests. At home, the parties would be conciliated into supporting a national programme to strengthen the state and defend it against social revolution. The package demonstrated an alarming failure to appreciate the deep conflicts at work within Germany and the complexities of Germany's international position.[5]

The non-renewal of the socialist laws – which had been one of Bismarck's first disagreements with William II – failed to conciliate the socialists, despite the improvement it brought them. One of the reasons was that the normal processes of the law were still used against them with the utmost rigour, and no apparent conciliation could make up for this disability. The SPD continued to grow in cohesion, numbers and organisation, and became in the Second International the greatest socialist party in Europe. Nor was the SPD impressed by the new labour legislation passed in July 1890. It consisted of the establishment of labour courts to deal with disputes between employee and employer, and a labour code – particularly the brainchild of William II – which so shifted the boundary between public and private concerns as to offend against liberal principles of minimal state interference with private enterprise. Somewhat more successful was the alteration of Bismarck's fixed tariff so as to make possible negotiation between the government and industry as to the suitable rate. It also allowed reciprocal negotiations to take place with other states and possibly, though by no means certainly, assisted the unprecedented expansion after 1895 in Germany's trade. Certainly Caprivi made bilateral trade treaties with many other countries and in so doing finally alienated the agrarians from the government. This was both an indication of the fact that it had only been temporary conditions that had induced them to support Bismarck's protection, and that Germany was now an industrial state whose main economic preoccupation must be with the health of her industry and no longer with the traditional interests of the eastern farming districts. So unconciliated were the landowners by this treatment that they took to the public stage – which must have been anathema to their Prussian souls – and campaigned for better treatment. They were anti-Semite, anti-socialist, and played upon the fears of the bourgeoisie of the south and the interests of the east. It was not a pretty omen for the future.

The policy of conciliation was not proving a success, and with its failure went failure in the Chancellor's usefulness to the Emperor – his ability to control the *Reichstag*. Further policies aimed at improving matters now began to be thrown out in the *Reichstag*. Tax reforms, for example, particularly in Prussia, were much needed, and could be a way of fulfilling the old Bismarckian goal of abolishing the state contribution to the Exchequer and replacing it with federal indirect taxation. Johannes von Miquel, who was in fact a National Liberal, became Prussian Minister for Finance in 1891 and at once began to change the basis of the Prussian revenue-collecting from land to incomes, thus increasing the yield by fairer means, and recognising a great social change. At the imperial level, however, Miquel encountered successful opposition, and what little reform he did succeed in, created much resentment in the conservative and liberal parties. So also did an attempt to put all the estates in Prussia under the local administrations. It is difficult to imagine, from a British point of view, that this could ever not have been so; the fact is, despite Caprivi's efforts in the early nineties, there were estates in Prussia which remained feudally controlled and were not subject to any local government. No institutions of local government appeared in the Prussian countryside until after the First World War.

Efforts to conciliate the centre were made by removing the last vestiges of the *Kulturkampf*, both in financial terms and in education. The Prussian Exchequer was still receiving the interest from monies it had confiscated from the Church, and in 1891 the government returned the whole sum. But over primary education a bill to strengthen the religious character and control over primary schools was strongly opposed by the National Liberals and all parties to the left of them, and actually divided the government. In March 1892 William II, no doubt fully conscious of the drama of the situation, called a Council of State, and insisted that the bill be modified so that it could be agreed at least by the government. Zedlitz-Trützschler, the Prussian Education Minister, resigned, thus leaving Caprivi without the support of the centre. The Chancellor then resigned also. This might have been a moment to assert the responsibility of the government to the *Reichstag* majority, had previous history been different, but in the end Caprivi withdrew his resignation, and the bill was withdrawn from the *Reichstag*. Conciliation had suffered, the Chancellor had suffered, the cause of education had suffered – nothing was done about primary education until 1918. But above all, despite his dramatic intervention the Emperor suffered. Having made his *démarche*, he then did nothing except leave Berlin on an extended hunting expedition during a week of constitutional crisis. The one actual result was disastrous: the Chancellor gave up the office of Minister-President of Prussia, which went to a strongly conservative protégé of the court, Botho von Eulenburg. Caprivi had become convinced that the Reich Chancellor should give up his responsibility within the Prussian Ministry of State and seek to establish himself as a purely Reich figure, whose relations with the non-Prussian parts of the empire would thereby be improved. In fact what he did both helped to wither the roots of the Chancellorship and inflamed William II's desire to rule in an absolute style. For, so far from welcoming Caprivi's changes, the non-Prussian parts of Germany had relied on the Chancellor's entrenched position in Prussia, as maintained by Bismarck, to guarantee them against Prussian encroachments; while if the Chancellor was to act as any sort of effective leader of the government, he had to stand on the firm base of the Prussian Ministry of State. Caprivi thus failed in his somewhat naïve plan, and became the victim of intrigue carried on both by the leaderless Prussian ministers and by the increasingly powerful court entourage, whose objective was to put William II in charge.[6]

It will be remembered also that lack of co-ordination between the imperial government such as it was and the government of Prussia had been relieved by the practice of allowing ministers to hold both Prussian and imperial offices – very often uniting the two functions. For no one was this more important than for the Chancellor, and now the two offices had been split. For the first time Prussian ministers and imperial secretaries began to speak with different voices. Had the imperial government been a strong thing, had the Emperor not been King of Prussia, this would have been a happy development – as it was, it was the beginning of what was to become an administrative impossibility.

As Caprivi became progressively discredited, the power of the Kaiser began to grow – a growth nurtured and to some extent planned by a group of courtiers, not least Philipp Eulenburg and Bernhard Bülow. They had a vision of a future government of Germany in which the Kaiser would decide what policy should be, and devoted able officials, like themselves, would carry it out. This was to be made possible by inserting the Kaiser's men into official positions, and so enhancing the Kaiser's prestige by successful foreign adventures that the pattern of politics in the Second Reich could be turned upside down with impunity.

As Dr Rohl has shown, in the three years between 1894 and 1897 this programme was carried out.[7] The new Chancellor, who had succeeded Caprivi in October 1894, was Hohenlohe, an aged Bavarian liberal. He did so against an extremely confused political background in which the markedly undemocratic franchise arrangement still in operation in Prussia had produced a considerable campaign on the left and thus stimulated a highly vocal, heavy-handedly nationalistic demand for repressive legislation. The Kaiser put himself at the head of this campaign. In the event, Hohenlohe was not able to introduce a return to a more stable condition, and not, as he said, wishing to trouble the Kaiser with his resignation over 'trivial' matters, he was gradually reduced to impotence – a straw Chancellor. The process concerned office-holders rather than policies, for whatever other uncertainties existed, there was no doubt that the Kaiser controlled appointments. The success of any Chancellor's administration had naturally depended on appointments being made which bore some relationship to the Chancellor's wishes and paid some attention to the likely effect of their policies on the *Reichstag*. After 1894, these considerations were abandoned in a complicated plot, largely conducted by Eulenburg and Bülow, to replace the Chancellor's nominees by imperial cronies. The occasions began to arise out of Hohenlohe's unwillingness to act as a buffer between the Kaiser and the Cabinet. This meant that the ministry came into direct contact with the imperial Cabinets, and predictably tried to make a stand on the basis of constitutional authority. This was, equally predictably, not acceptable to the Kaiser and his entourage, and as the Chancellor, against his own judgement, began to accept imperially acceptable ministers, first violent disagreements developed between the two sides in the Cabinet, and then in 1897 with the appointments of Tirpitz as Naval Secretary, Bülow as Foreign Secretary and Posadowsky as Prussian Minister of the Interior, the entire Reich administration was in the hands of the Kaiser's men. 'The fact is,' he recorded, 'I have lost my authority over the Kaiser and thus my *raison d'être.'*[8] He was decidedly right about the former; but as a sleeping Chancellor he had not lost his *raison d'être*, and he remained in office until replaced by Bülow in 1900.

With the new regime of 1897, a fresh development began to show itself at the centre of German government. Both in appearance and in practice the Reich Chancellorship had been seriously devalued. It had been so partly because the office itself was not constitutionally manageable, but partly and more obviously because the Kaiser possessed a strong wish to rule without restraint, and had been able to achieve with the help of his closest private associates something not far short of his ideal. There was no doubt that it would be possible for a Kaiser to rule in this way, provided that he could find a sufficiently self-effacing Chancellor, and provided that he was politically skilful, consistent in his behaviour and a character of weight. William II had none of these characteristics as has been seen. Not only did he lack them, he possessed other debilitating qualities not the least of which was his tendency to extreme and often laughable public utterances. This, together with his known tendency to work with a shifting body of court favourites, brought the central office of the Reich into disrepute. More or less at the same moment, both the great executive offices of state were for different reasons much lowered in their political effect and indeed in public esteem.

II

Almost as if the gods intended troubles for Germany, the collapse of tight controls at the centre coincided with the opening of her period of greatest power, and of the greatest tension, both internally and externally. She went through a period of unprecedented trading and industrial expansion, with all the social pressures that this involved, and found herself rapidly becoming encircled as other powers became frightened and looked to their own security.

The topics which must now concern us are interconnected, and of cumulative significance: economic expansion, leading to social unrest, a new navy, and an over-vigorous foreign policy. It is worth remembering that those theorists who wrote so persistently about imperialism and the development of capitalist societies around this time, did so on the basis of their analysis of the German experience. Thus one is apt to be impressed by the accuracy of both analysis and forecast, and possibly to be as ready as they were to extrapolate the results into a general theory: of this one should beware. It is, however, equally true that the results observed by Lenin and Hobson are not invalidated by the uses to which they were put and if we find the last stages of capitalism being enacted before our eyes, it must be accepted as the German situation.[9]

Imperialism had been given a new meaning by Lenin, that of exploitation, and a new explanation, as the outcome of money, surplus capital at home, pressing for investment abroad. This in turn was explained as the consequence of cartelisation in industry, the concentration of banking and the monopoly of economic power by relatively few financiers. All these factors came into existence during the Bismarckian period, as it was observable that financiers were beginning 'to determine where the politicians should act and which of their actions should bear fruit'.[10]

Rising population was the most striking feature of Germany's developments: between 1870 and 1890, it rose from 41 million to 49 million, which was a spectacular rise; but from 1890 to 1915 it rose to nearly 70 million, which was phenomenal. France, for example, only crept up to 40 million during the First World War. The extra population provided a greater labour supply and a larger market. The currency remained stable, and incomes generally rose: economic expansion seemed preordained and permanent.

The main flow of population was to the cities, which grew into great conurbations unlike anything else in Germany – or Europe. The flight from the land was a consequence of the industrial growth in Germany and mounted steadily. In 1895, for example, 35 per cent of the population still lived in rural areas, as against 8 per cent in Britain, and therefore there was plenty of labour left in the pool to equip the expansion after 1900. This last can be seen if we observe the figures – expressed in millions of tons – of the three primary industries. Coal production rose between 1870 and 1890, by steady leaps from 34 to 149; but from 1900 to 1910 it rose to 222 and had reached 277 by 1914. The same sudden expansion can be seen in iron production: from 1870 to 1890 it rose steadily from 1.3 to 6.7, after which it jumped in ten years to 13.1 in 1900, reaching 14 in 1914. It was the same story with steel, though of even greater importance since steel was a vitally competitive area in international trade: from 1870 to 1900, the figures rose from 0.3 to 6.7, but from 1900 to 1910 they rose to 13.8 and to 14 in 1914. Simple production-level figures also tell the same story, although here the major expansion came ten years earlier. From 1891 to 1895, production increased by 40 per cent – the largest increase in imperial history – and matched by an increase in Britain of only 15 per cent. From 1896 to 1900 there was a 21 per cent rise, whereas in Britain it was 4 per cent. After 1900 the figures are unreliable, but show nevertheless a continuing rise.[11]

What we have to observe particularly about this expansion is not only the staggering amount, as shown by the major industries, but the general direction which it was taking. For although protection had given an artificial boost to primary products, it had not altered what would have been an even more marked development without it, namely the expansion of the new technological industries, which was where the greatest hole in the international market lay. This was the field where Germany completely outstripped her neighbours, particularly Britain; in chemical industries, engineering, precision-tool making, and electrical apparatus of all sorts, Germany assumed the leading positions in the world. And this was a world wherein the possession of such skills brought results beyond the ordinary rewards of hard work and skilful selling. Such exportable products made German industry competitive in every part of the world, and saw a great German penetration into extra-European areas hitherto supplied, albeit clumsily, by the British. The result was a formidable increase of commercial activity in extra-European fields, particularly railway construction.

From this followed a social situation which needs to be examined. The appearance of social problems did not long await the arrival of the new Chancellor. The first problem was one of a conflict renewed between the landed and industrial interests. Bülow's solution was to frame a new measure of protection putting a five-mark duty on grain. He wanted to reduce the swing towards industry which the economy had taken, lessen the flight from the land where the place of German-peasants was being taken by immigrant Poles, peg the value of land, and maintain food supplies for the urban areas. The new measure was a most complex law of some thousand clauses, which finally passed the *Reichstag* in 1905, after three years of negotiations. It was a measure of Bülow's skill that such a bill, supported by different groups in different sections, should have got through at all. The end result, however, was a further quarrel between the two interests, and in the election of 1903 the government was heavily censured by all parties, particularly the SPD. They claimed that a slight rise in prices after 1900 had left the working man in need of help. Bülow's answer was a bill to help widows and orphans, and legislation dealing with the right of association, removing disabilities from the Jesuits, and the prohibition on affiliated societies. Members of the *Reichstag* were paid for the first time – some few years it might be noted before MPs in Britain (1911). None of these measures dealt with matters of real complaint like the franchise laws – particularly of Prussia, which still retained its antique system or the need to redraw the constituency boundaries.

It was issues such as these which brought the SPD into increasing prominence. It was growing vastly as a party, and the great revisionism controversy enabled it to be somewhat less stereotyped in its political behaviour, and more willing to employ some of the devices which others had used to keep it from its rightful strength. At the same time, there was a great growth in the number and importance of the trade unions. A struggle with the industrial employers' league in 1890 had caused the setting-up of a national general commission, which co-ordinated trade union activity on a national scale, induced centralisation and gave a lead on political questions. By 1906, the unions were wealthy and powerful and offering services on a wide range. They were far more numerous in their membership than the SPD. As might be expected in an industrial community which had become so centralised, employers were not slow, nor less effective, in forming leagues of their own; and around the turn of the century the prevalence of strikes had caused employers to accumulate enormous funds, which had made them able to withstand any stoppages. The appearance of these great employers' groups, together with the old landowners' league made them a yet more powerful force in politics. To demand control of labour was one thing; to be able to enforce it was regrettably quite another matter.

This stalemate did not end the struggle, and the winter of 1905/6 saw further outbreaks. A Belgian strike in 1902 had given rise to new thinking about the general strike as a weapon of great effectiveness, and the Russian Revolution of 1905 had put new ideas and new heart into the German working-men's organisations. In January to February 1905, the Ruhr miners' strike was more widely spontaneous and more far-reaching in its demands than it would have been without the Russian Revolution. The important concessions which followed gave added impetus to plans for an improved organisation so that mass strikes could become generally effective. The mass strike as a political weapon seemed to have become a practical proposition. Extremists in the SPD, with support from the unions, had a resolution adopted in the party congress at Jena during September 1905, which recommended the mass strike as a formidable line of defence for the working class. Rosa Luxemburg, now in a splinter group of the SPD, provided a rallying cry and a technique in her *General Strike: Parties and Unions*. Quite soon a great suffrage crisis tried out the seriousness of the party's intentions. In the trade unions, conservative members had tried at the conference of 1905 to prevent the discussion of mass strikes, but had been overruled; would the unions be as vigorous as the SPD claimed that it would be? The traditions of united Germany do not allow of doubt in the answer. They failed; but nevertheless the crisis was serious.

Late in 1905, agitation broke out in Saxony for electoral reform, where in the late nineties the franchise had been suddenly narrowed for fear of a future SPD state majority. Workers took to the streets in Dresden, Chemnitz and Plauen, demanding a repeal of the reactionary law of 1896 and the establishment of universal direct suffrage and the secret ballot. On 21 January 1906 there were protest meetings throughout Germany and the movement was at its height. But the SPD decided that it did not want to get out of step with the unions and the two sides of the movement agreed to present a repudiation of the general strike to the congress at Mannheim in March 1906. Nevertheless the unions had shown their power, and popular unrest had not reached such heights before in the Second Reich. The effect, as Bülow admitted in his memoirs, was to make the government seek for external nationalist circuses to keep the population amused. The social crisis in Germany could not be solved within the terms of the existing constitution. The ruling élite had done a deal with industrialists and with the bourgeoisie by which the political structures of Germany had been weakened, so that power was exercised by one element which cared for position, in favour of another party which cared for influence. Now, no new deals could be made with the workers, nor could they be allowed to inject reality into the political system. As in other sectors of German life an impasse had been reached, and it was only a matter of time before an explosion came.

This crisis was deeper even than that caused by the collapse of responsible government in the face of the determination of the court to see the Kaiser rule untrammelled. The coup of 1897 was the end of a struggle for power within the constitutional structure which began with the dismissal of Bismarck; but it did not change the relationship between the constitution of 1871 and the new Germany of the 1890s. Indeed it strengthened the Prussian element in the government, since that was the inevitable court bias. Bismarck had recognised that some accommodation had to be arranged between the need to protect united Germany from political changes which might upset the dominant position of the Prussian landowning classes, and the needs of the growing industrial state. National Germany had been created to guarantee the stability of Prussia; but national Germany had quickly been overtaken by industrial

Germany. The primary concerns of Reich government ought to have become the problems and needs of a new industrial society. And the men to do the job ought to have come increasingly, as in other European states, from the leaders of that society. But they did not. The process that Bismarck had begun at the time of his change to protection went further during the reign of William II. The great bankers, industrialists and traders from the Ruhr, from Hamburg, and in Berlin were successfully excluded both from high society and from governmental office. They were persuaded not to seek the proper representation of the new Germany by being given the shadow of power, and by the offer of protection from the socialists. Fear of socialism made the *haute bourgeoisie* to which these leaders belonged reluctant to lead any demands for the liberalisation of political machinery; they feared the consequences of associating with socially inferior people, and the possibility that such changes would not stop short of revolution. It was easier for them to acquiesce in their exclusion from the seats of social and political power when they could convince themselves that the regime did not really need reform. By the time that Wilhelmine Germany was firmly set on the road to war, it was too late for successful protest. The influence that they wielded had seemed great – perhaps greater for the mystique which surrounded the private ways in which it was brought to bear. It was also, in purely economic terms, successful. It was possible for men like Albert Ballin, who was a great shipping magnate, to ignore the need for reform, because his desires were largely met and he could feel that he was an influence in Berlin. He and his like were an influence, but they were not more; and the regime they influenced was unstable. Because their largely economic influence was important at Berlin, these commercial kings not only believed that the regime did not need reform, they also overestimated the extent of their political influence. William II, unlike his court circle generally, loved the attentions which men of wealth happily showered on him, and so far from giving the attentive visitors more influence over him, such fulsome service merely increased William's imperviousness to sound advice. They had gained an entrée to the court and the government by the back door, and when they realised that the shadow of power was insufficient to avert political and economic disaster, it was too late. They believed in social stability and international peace; they could not see that in emasculating themselves to secure the former, they merely made the latter less likely. The events in 1897 put into power the men who believed in *Weltpolitik*, and the great fleet; only the influence of private pressure-groups or revolution could now stop them. In the battle for influence, it was the Kaiser's men who won. In 1915, Albert Ballin, one of the most political of industrialists, wrote sorrowfully:

> My ships did not need the protection of a German fleet, and I should have emphatically said so to the Kaiser. But I could never summon the courage to do so.... Among his pet projects, the fleet was the greatest. Now we have the result of our lack of courage.[12]

III

In now considering the navy, we come to the connecting link between Germany's internal problems and external policies. Unquestionably the decision to build a High Seas fleet taken in 1897 affected the history of the Reich more importantly than any other during the period of the empire, with the exception of the constitutional decisions of the 1860s and in 1870. For it changed fundamentally the basis of German foreign policy and made it face west, out to the sea, as well as landwards; and it brought upon Germany the enmity of Britain.

In a curious way, the decision to build a great fleet, and the persistence shown by every German government in maintaining its progress, despite the failure of the policy which it was intended to initiate, brings out most significantly the ills that lay at the root of German society and politics. It has been regarded in the past as an example of what can happen when technology gets out of control. Indeed it must be one of the first historical developments to be so regarded. Men as the prisoners of their machines is a doctrine which rightly takes account of the enormous importance of technological advance of naval matters, but ignores the quite deliberate way in which Grand Admiral Tirpitz justified his expansion, and the quite rational way in which a disastrous policy was presented to the public and to the *Reichstag*. Nor is it the case that the navy was an unforgivable outbreak of German militarism. At least two German historians of the period of Tirpitz – Hubatsch and Gerhard Ritter[13] – viewed the naval expansion in this light – Ritter more understandably so since he was writing about the tradition of *militarismus*. In Tirpitz they seemed to have found their model. But to say this ignores the entirely rational purpose of Tirpitz's policy. Tirpitz believed, and it was not an unreasonable belief, that in view of Britain's resources and attitudes she would surely prefer alliance with Germany either to financial ruin or to unpalatable agreements with her traditional enemies France or Russia. Naval rivalry ought to be the most effective method of bringing this about.

So, if the naval race was entered upon for an observable political policy, it still leaves the question, why did the navy become so popular, why, in fact, did the plan succeed, even to the point of getting out of control and contravening the very policy it had been designed to pursue? One explanation is the undoubted fact that the Kaiser believed in the navy policy, with a fervour and persistence that was denied to many another scheme. Holstein wrote that inability to brook opposition and the plan to create a navy equal to Britain's were 'the two principles to which the Kaiser remained true throughout his reign'.[14] In this he was in some ways running true to form: when he urged the navy policy on his people he was to some extent following opinion rather than making it. As new modern states have felt the necessity for a prestige airline of their own, at whatever ludicrous cost, so a respectable navy was the nineteenth-century equivalent. Moreover, the fact was that Germany had to keep up with the latest naval technology if she were to remain a great power. If it was inevitable that the Kaiser should be demanding a navy for these reasons it may also be remarked that what we know of his curious attitude to Britain made it inevitable that he should see it in a British context; and to be fair, it does seem as if naval matters appealed to him, as model railways appeal to other people. His delight in it all was both infectious and dangerous, and his support for the schemes of Admirals Senden and Tirpitz was an important element in their success. Dr Steinberg has written:

> The unusual position of the German navy in the society of Imperial Germany gave it great sources of strength. No other German or Prussian institution could call on the same associations with the nationalist movement. In a new nation state as yet uncertain about its style, structure and identity, the navy was unequivocally national and imperial. It had no particularist or states' rights in existence to obstruct its growth. It could claim an honourable liberal past and appeal to the rising industrial and commercial classes as a thoroughly middle class organisation.[15]

No one who does not understand that the army was kept firmly within the control of the old Prussian aristocracy, propagating its distasteful ideas and promoting only its members, can appreciate the opposition always encountered in the *Reichstag* when the army was under discussion, nor its reluctance to increase that which it did not control.[16] The navy was imperial, dependent on the *Reichstag* for its very existence.

Its ideas were the ideas of the trading classes, its officers were members of it. To many radicals it offered the universal panacea of colonial expansion and settlement, which, they believed, would ease if not solve domestic social problems. To the economists and historians it seemed the perfect instrument for the fulfilment of their neo-mercantilist or social-Darwinian theories of international relations. It could carry German *Kultur* to every corner of the globe and wrest for Germany that place among nations for which the German academic community believed she had been historically destined. Thus Bülow in the *Reichstag* said in 1897:

> We do not by any means feel the need to stick our fingers in every pie, but on the other hand . . . the days when the German happily surrendered the land to one of his neighbours, to another the sea, and reserved for himself the heavens, where pure doctrine was enthroned . . . (laughter) those days are over. In a word, we don't want to put any one else in the shade, but we too demand a place in the sun.[17]

Of course there were also great handicaps to be overcome, which taxed Tirpitz's administrative and political qualities to the utmost, but he had strong forces with him, and outstanding abilities himself. In 1898, the Navy Law was passed through the *Reichstag*, by considerable majorities, and that House was never to refuse the navy anything it wanted until the war of 1914.

If there was any justification for a German navy above trivial size, it lay in the view that Germany's foreign trade had made her commerce such a vital feature of the economy that means had to be available to prevent a blockade of her coasts – which must have been the obvious tactic of an enemy – and to protect her traders in faraway places. But this was not what the planners of the navy intended: they intended a threat to Britain. Admiral Senden, Tirpitz's predecessor, was convinced that, contrary to the general line of German policy, Britain was the real power with which she had to reckon, and had sufficiently persuaded the Kaiser of this. Tirpitz elaborated such vague intimations into a theory of policy, which he clearly set out in the preamble to the Navy Bill. It was, incidentally, one of the reasons why the *Reichstag* passed naval legislation without much cavil, that the Naval Office always stated clearly what their intention and strategy was. This theory was known, and has attained notoriety, as the Risk Theory, and its straightforward publication merely added to the suspicions that the British were bound to feel. The idea was that the British must be persuaded to make terms with Germany, and to encourage her to do so she was to be threatened by the appearance of a powerful German fleet, stationed in the North Sea, between Heligoland and the Thames. Such a fleet would also prevent what was a persistent chimera in German thinking, the danger of a sudden punitive expedition by the British across the North Sea. 'The risk theory was both an offensive and defensive strategy, a lever and a deterrent' (Steinberg).[18] It was also a startling commentary on the times, and on Tirpitz's intelligence that the employment of technologically advanced force was being used to secure a diplomatic result. After 1900 the lever against Britain began to work, and to work in precisely the opposite way to that intended. The expansion of the German navy in the North Sea increased the chance of a British attack; every extra risk for Britain was in turn an extra risk for Germany, because the result was not to push Britain into the arms of Germany, but to draw all the other powers together, until finally Germany was faced with the appalling possibility of war on two fronts and war against the greatest naval power at the same time. But as has been seen, the navy had a very particular place in the life of Germany, and a particular meaning for her; even when the plan had failed, the treadmill could not be stopped. Wilhelmine Germany possessed one truly national institution: it symbolised what the new German middle class could not secure from its accommodation with the Prussian establishment. It was liberal, open to the bourgeoisie, nationalist and commercial. It was tragically also a central point in Anglo-German hostility.

The strategy was neither foolish, nor wicked, nor inevitably doomed to failure. But it rested on a new assumption about German foreign policy. 'The German Empire has become a world power', declared the Kaiser at one stage, and although he confused a desire with an accomplished fact, he expressed this assumption well. If Germany was to become a world power, she had at least to challenge Britain. If she was seeking security, even hegemony in Europe, she did not need to. The only road to success against Britain involved a policy of extreme caution with other powers. But men who were determined upon seizing world power were not able to do so with finesse. They could not understand that the naval policy absolutely depended upon quiescence; that no other power must be frightened into friendship with Britain before she had come to Berlin. And as the traditions of Germany aided the naval programme, so other pressures within Germany rendered a suitable foreign policy impossible. After the passage of the Navy Bill in 1898, the vicious circle was drawn tighter and tighter. Bismarck's foreign policy had been skilfully arranged to avoid the dangers inherent in Germany's weak strategic position, and was concerned to strengthen the European system of international relations, established after the Congress of Vienna. His successors led by the new Kaiser saw less of the difficulties in Germany's position, and more of her great and increasing power. They abandoned the treaty with Russia, relaxed restraint on Austria, and pursued a policy of bluster all around the world. In so doing they created an unfavourable situation, and this made them more aggressive than they already were. For having such great power, they sought European hegemony as of right, and intended to use it to give Germany security in a future community of world powers. But a foreign policy of bluster and a naval policy of expansion were incompatibles, and so frightened other powers that they either converted old agreements into anti-German coalitions or built up new ones. In the face of the German crisis, they were prepared to abandon considerations that the Germans had relied upon to keep them apart, and this fact threw such calculations as Berlin had made into confusion.

At the same time the internal situation, which had seemed to improve briefly after 1897, began to deteriorate sharply at the turn of the century. The existing distribution of political power came to be increasingly questioned, whether through discussions of the constitutional position of the *Reichstag*, the operation of anachronistic systems of voting, or through the campaigns of the trade union movement. Against these developments, the customary techniques of appeasement were failing to work. Neither the first nor second Morocco crises induced a smoother water in domestic affairs and, particularly the Agadir crisis, did not succeed in influencing the outcome of the subsequent general election. Nor did the peremptory tone of German diplomacy produce any improvement in her international position – indeed, it appeared to be steadily worsening. Defence policy was beginning to give rise to new and uncomfortable developments. It was plain that a naval policy of expansion would have to give way before the competitive necessities imposed by the military policies of France and Russia. To reduce the pace of shipbuilding, apart from being an admission of the failure of Tirpitz's policy, was also to cause economic despondency amongst a broad spectrum of German industry. To expand the army provided no compensating domestic bonus. So far from giving an economic stimulus, it meant approaching the *Reichstag* for highly unpopular additional taxation. The inequitable way in which the burden of taxation fell upon different sections of the population had for long been one of the prized advantages of the groups in power and one of the great complaints of the opposition: to have to increase taxation was certain to create great political discomfort, and perhaps to create hopes of reform which were not and could not be realised. In addition, to increase the size of the army must mean recruiting a larger number of possibly disaffected ordinary soldiers, on whom a great deal of political 'education' would have to be imposed, and the commissioning of officers from outside the ruling élite.[19]

In addition to the general development of difficulties for Germany, both internally and externally, there were also quite precise political storms, which tended to bring the constitutional arrangements of the Reich into disrepute. The effect of the *Daily Telegraph* affair in 1908, which followed the publication in the London *Daily Telegraph* of a highly indiscreet interview with William II was both to lower further the standing of the Kaiser, and to bring to desperation those to whom the Crown was the symbol of the existing constitutional order. In the case of the Zabern affair, the effect was similar. In 1913, a young army officer stationed in the little Alsatian town of Zabern (Saverne) behaved very stupidly over a minor incident and ended by assaulting an ordinary citizen, after which there were some civil disorders. It is perhaps symbolic of both the nervousness and loss of a sense of proportion which characterised the German administration at the time that the whole apparatus of the German government was mobilised to support the officer concerned, leading to a great outcry and a virulent debate in the *Reichstag*. In the end, the failure of the Chancellor successfully to defend the army – and therefore the Kaiser – and the consequent demands for reform, caused an increase in the despairing attitude of the ruling class. With this came an increase in the number who were beginning to think that control over the apparatus of the state, still complete, might not long remain so, and should therefore be used to establish an unshakeable regime while the possibility remained. To the opposition, the devastatingly clear way in which the affair revealed the powerlessness of the civil administration in the face of the military Cabinet was an obvious justification for their campaign for reform. Once again, as in 1897, there was widespread talk of a *coup d'état*; and for those who had come to believe that the advance of the SPD and the trade unions had now made this impossible, there began to develop talk of a prophylactic war: an external war might do what no internal manipulation, either attempted or proposed, could do and bring about the reunification of German society under the Crown.

Both internally and externally, it looked as though the last moment had come. The economy was faltering under the weight of the armaments programme; in addition, a tariff war began with Russia in 1913. After the elections of 1912, it looked as though the state structure might not long survive. German military predominance in relation to the powers of the Triple Entente – supposing that combination to be a militarily coherent one – appeared to be on the wane. Germany's only serious ally, Austria–Hungary, was widely thought to be slipping rapidly towards extinction.

In these circumstances, it is possible to understand the gloomy depression that so much marked the attitude of Germans in government circles. It may have been reinforced by the strikingly circumscribed world, both in its size and in its atmosphere, in which the rulers of Germany moved. But their overall estimate was not wrong, given the preoccupations with internal and external security which they had. Above all, however, the existence of this kind of atmosphere, though it could not be decisive in its own right, helps to explain why the German government reacted to the crisis in 1914 as it did.[20]

IV

Until recent years, it has been easier to make a connection between domestic and foreign pressures and their effect on the foreign policy of Austria than of Germany. This can be seen particularly clearly during the Bosnia crisis of 1908–9, the Balkan Wars in 1912–13 and, again, in 1914. The weakness and decay of the Habsburg Empire was a matter of discussion and speculation at the time, and formed a part not only of the basic conditions of Austrian policy, but also of the calculations of the other powers, not least her principal ally, Germany. Moreover, in the case of Serbia, there seemed to be at stake both the authority of the state in a general way, and the quite precise problem of stopping what appeared to be the unending disaffection deliberately created by Serbian agency in the south-western parts of the empire. For both these reasons, it seemed as if Austria could not have been expected to avoid punishing Serbia in 1914.

Thus it seems quite right to ask why the Habsburg Empire had arrived at such a position; even, perhaps, whether contemporary and later negative assessments were just. It is perfectly possible to make up a balance sheet, as Jaszi did, and assess the relative force of the factors which tended to break up the monarchy and those which tended to preserve it.[21] But it is difficult to do this satisfactorily because, as he himself admits, some factors pulled both ways at the same time. The universalist parties, the Christian Socialists and the Social Democrats, had one effect under one leadership and with uneducated support, but produced precisely the opposite effect under newer leaders and with educated support. This was because the advent of a more general literacy transformed the nature of national aspirations and gave them a place among what had been markedly centripetal forces. None the less, it is remarkable that even at the end of the period, the nationalities were seeking self-advancement under the monarchy, not as its heirs. 'The game of *rouge et noir* was played', as Taylor remarks, 'on the Imperial table',[22] and yet it is clear that however willing the peoples were to live with the monarchy, the monarchy could not live with them. And it is too subjective to say *would* not. There can be no doubt that Francis Joseph would not tolerate real national gains, but it is clearer to us than it was to his advisers that he could not either. It is clear too that the *Ausgleich* of 1867, by which Hungary achieved final independence, although it was impossible to preserve the monarchy on any other terms when it was made, contained within itself the seeds of a longer-term destruction. For Hungarian interests were not Habsburg interests, yet they had achieved the dominant voice. In the end the most severe national crisis came in an area over which the monarchy did not have control, and proved to be unable to take control, in 1906.

Thus, it seems to be more worthwhile to try to take stock of the basic factors of the situation. The monarchy was the personal property of the Emperor, who drew his title from that fact, and not from any other relationship he may have had with his peoples. The official title of the empire was 'the peoples and lands represented in the *Reichsrat*' (imperial parliament), and that in itself reveals two different kinds of ownership. Some areas were held by feudal lords owing service on them to the Habsburgs, some were held directly: either way the possibility of a state and government relationship was precluded. This fact is the key with which other problems may be unlocked. The political effects in the eighteenth century were on the whole beneficent, in the nineteenth they were fatal. For the Emperor derived an attitude towards government from his patrimony that was wholly anachronistic, and a practice of politics which was a mixture of cunning and appeasement. He could not believe that any arrangement which did not leave him in sole and total control of his domains was anything but temporary and he operated on that basis. Thus it was neither possible to develop an Austrian idea nor possible to develop a stable political method that might at least have hidden the lack of any state concept. Both have been by themselves castigated as the cause of Habsburg downfall, and both have been regretted as omissions that might have been rectified. They were not so much causes as symptoms, and they were symptoms of the simple fact that the Habsburgs possessed no other authority than that given them by their dynasty and their lands. They were no longer Holy Roman Emperors, nor were they Emperors in Germany, nor were they Emperors of Austria; they were gigantic landlords who would make any and every repair rather than pull down the family mansion. If they surrendered their authority to a state, and ruled with its consent, they lost all. If they accepted an Austrian mission to reconcile the nationalities and preside over a multi-national empire, they opened the way to a constitution, a responsible ministry and, once again, they lost. They could not risk losing their own in return for the shadowy possibility of continued rule over an empire which only *might* not fall apart. Thus they became dependent on prestige to hold the line against the modern world, thereby becoming committed to a vigorous foreign policy which their strategic situation forbade as much as their internal weakness. And this very weakness was the result of their self-imposed policies.

The other side of the coin was an attitude to all reform, to every constitutional change which rendered it temporary. The governments of Bach and Schmerling, Hohenwart and Schäffle, Taaffe and Körber, all pursued opposed policies in quick succession, which were temporary expedients dressed up as final solutions. No concession could not be contemplated, because no concession was real. In 1908, the empire was in precisely similar case as it had been in 1849, only worse, and it was worse because confidence in the possibility of finding an idea for existence or a stable constitution which the Emperor would defend had dwindled to nothing. Stable government was one vital basis for a vigorous foreign policy, and it was lacking: economic efficiency and administrative care were others. In a world of modern states, which were both efficiently governed through technical improvements acquired during the great period of *laissez-faire*, and dependent for their power on the technological advances of their industries, Austria was lacking direction and the regime stultified development. She turned her administration into a national battleground for privilege, on a scale which is reminiscent of the way other countries had once tolerated the sale of offices; her industry, though existent, was discouraged by inbuilt economic factors and confined to one small area of the country. There was no inducement to follow the Emperor into battle, nothing to fight for, even, for some, defeat to be hoped for; while there was simply not the sheer power available to support grandiose schemes in Germany, Hungary, the Balkans or anywhere else.

The consequences of the imperial position, however, were not as serious as the strongest force with which it collided. It is the greatest irony of the situation that the monarchy which could not have faced the concept of nationalism in one people alone was destined to be the most subject to its ravages among many. Both doctrines of nationalism and liberalism would have been difficult to reconcile with the monarchy, even had it been prepared to treat its lands as a state. As it was, the one led to federalism and the other to a permanent constitution, both to the devolution of authority: neither could be tolerated. So the heavy hand of bureaucracy was multiplied to serve national ambitions, and the monarchy conceded when it had to and withdrew concessions when it could. After 1867, the unitary solution, hitherto unlikely because of the state structure and ethos it would bring, was in any case impossible. Probably if any solution was possible, that alone could have achieved it, but not in the nineteenth century. The ultimate effect of the *Ausgleich* was also to prevent, even if it had not been doomed by Habsburg needs, any form of federal solution. Hungary would allow neither a unitary state nor a federal state and, perforce, the Habsburgs agreed with them.

These by themselves would have amounted to deep crises; together they were insurmountable and for all that favourable historians have pointed to the growth of the proletariat, to the spread of the railways, to the increase of education, to the common army and to the great free trade area which the empire created; for all that the aristocracy, the Church, the bureaucracy, industrialists and the dynasty itself were unifying factors, they can only take credit for preserving the empire against all the odds for over a hundred years.[23]

By 1908, temporary solutions had run out, and the monarchy was effectively governed by a combination of the threat of military force and purely bureaucratic processes. Certainly, if the main obstacle to progress, the 1867 settlement, was to be removed, it would only be done as the consequence of victory in war; as will be seen, Hungarian consciousness of that fact affected their behaviour in February 1909 and July 1914.

The maturing of the domestic crisis of the monarchy coincided with the maturing of the general international crisis brought about by the Russo-Japanese War and the Anglo-Russian Convention of 1907. The next major upheaval – the Bosnia crisis of 1908–9 – was to be the first purely European crisis for twenty years, the most serious before the First World War and had been directly induced by the policy of Austria. The events of July 1914, if not directly the consequence of Austrian action, concerned her no less, and the course and nature of the crisis were profoundly affected by the internal compulsions of Germany working upon the evident necessities of the Austrian situation.

Further Reading

M. Balfour, *The Kaiser and His Times* (Cresset, 1964).

H. Böhme, *An Introduction to the Economic and Social History of Germany* (Oxford: Blackwell, 1978).

F. Fischer, *War of Illusions* (Chatto & Windus, 1975).

O. Jaszi, *The Dissolution of the Hapsburg Empire* (Chicago, 1928).

C. A. Macartney, *The Hapsburg Empire, 1790–1918* (Weidenfeld and Nicolson, 1968).

A. Ramm, *Germany 1789–1919* (Methuen, 1967).

J. C. G. Rohl, *Germany without Bismarck* (Batsford, 1967).

J. Steinberg, *Yesterday's Deterrent* (Macdonald, 1965).

A. J. P. Taylor, *Bismarck, the Man and the Statesman* (Hamish Hamilton, 1955).

——, *The Hapsburg Monarchy* (Peregrine, 1964).

4. The Role of Technological Change

If it is comparatively easy to demonstrate that two of the conditions permitting the functioning of the Concert of Europe had been gravely damaged by 1902 – the defined area and an even distribution of power – it is less easy to describe satisfactorily those more general factors which also contributed to international discomfort and unease. Most of them spring in one way or another from the extensive spread of industrialisation and its concomitant or in some cases consequential technological change. Perhaps the most profound effects were felt in changes in the distribution of power. This can be seen in terms of creating a new kind of disequilibrium between the developed world – largely in Europe – and the less developed world, and doing so at the same moment when for the same reasons, but differently deployed, a great advance occurred in the sophistication of communications.[1] Such an effect is plainly to be seen in the history of the Far East at the end of the century. The new order of technological development had a destructive effect upon the old, and induced conditions which advanced states found intolerable and possessed the means to rectify by influence, or eventually control. Then, again, as the international situation came to seem threateningly uncertain, the prospect of relief, or the compulsion to remove doubt by pre-emptive occupation, held out temptations to states which this world disequilibrium both caused and encouraged.

In European terms, the advance of the industrial revolution and the change in its character which greater technological skills brought about had complicated effects within Europe itself. It is commonly noted that the particular characteristic of the great German industrial and commercial advances of the late nineteenth century was its technological base, and it is certainly true that the enormous pace and success of German economic growth owed much to this factor.[2] It is also commonly noted that the advances of the German economy created for her a preponderance of power in Europe, which taken together with the rapid rise in her population and her concentration upon creating and maintaining armaments, caused a breakdown in the long-established parity of power amongst the European great powers. (See chapter 3.)

But this factor, though obvious, was not the only effect of this general change. If it caused a positive effect in respect of Germany, it also created a negative effect upon the British economy. It was not simply that Germany added her own advance to the stock of European economic activity, which of itself created a competition for raw materials and markets; there was in addition an absolute decline in British economic performance. This decline exceeded what was inevitable in the face of increasing competition from the very much larger economic base now appearing in the United States, or was perhaps to be expected as a result of the demographic revolution in Germany. It was rendered more serious and more rapid by the peculiar opportunity, eagerly seized, which lay open to Britain because of her past predominance, to ignore a collapse in industrial production and pay for her imports out of invisible earnings. It was an effective cloak, but it did not change the reality of decline, nor did it prevent worried politicians of the turn of the century from seeking imperial federation or other protectionist panaceas with which to halt the process. In terms of competition with Germany the effect was to emphasise the failure of the British to invest in their own industries or to develop new technologies. In the latter case, the British were falling behind in just the area where the possession of new, highly complex, technology was the point where economic performance had its greatest effect on the vital question of the distribution of international power.[3]

Other European states were also affected. One of the reasons for the decline in the viability of the Habsburg Empire as a state – let alone as a great power – was that her progress towards developing a modern industrial economy was much slower than that of other powers. The same could long be said of Russia, until in the early years of the century she entered upon a period of sharply quickening economic growth – a factor which came powerfully to influence German policy by 1913–14.[4]

Technological considerations also affected the military stalemate which was such an important feature of the international situation in the late nineteenth century. Stockpiling armaments has not only been a characteristic of the cold war. As technological advances rendered war offices more and more ready to spend large sums on research and then to adopt the results thus achieved, so the quality of guns improved. The apotheosis of all guns was realised with the construction of Big Bertha, of

First World War fame. But while it was possible to design improved guns almost endlessly, and to produce them in enormous quantities, it was not yet possible to deploy them effectively in battle. The consequence was that European governments became obsessed by the sheer size of their armies and the amount of their stockpiled weaponry. In part, this development was caused by the gradual erosion of international security, occurring for different reasons, but it was also in itself partly a cause of increasing anxiety and tension.

The reason for this failure to make these new and immense weapons mobile is to be found in the different pace at which technological improvement occurred in different areas of activity. Until 1917 it was possible to move big guns only on trains, with all the strategically limiting effects which naturally followed, and while governments could and did build thousands of miles of strategic railways, no one could guarantee that a future war would be fought in an appropriate place. Not until the petrol engine was sufficiently reliable to be applied to military purposes, and the resulting armoured vehicles mass-produced, was this stalemate broken.

On the sea, however, the application of the steam engine had been immediately successful. On water the steamship was mobile, and on the water the new arts of technologically advanced weapon-construction could have their effect. In short, the only area of potential war operations where there was no stalemate was at sea. Even had no other factors entered into the situation, this must have affected the relations between naval or potential naval powers, and where other factors brought about a conflict of interest between two seafaring states, it made certain that the political and strategic vocabulary of that conflict must be naval.

Anglo-German naval rivalry as it developed after 1900 provides an example of this effect, as it does of other factors discussed in the previous chapter.[5] It also provides a more detailed example of the dramatic effect of the introduction of a new piece of advanced technology. The German naval programme had originally been intended to push the British Empire into an alliance with Germany, by offering what could ultimately be only a theoretical menace to British safety. For reasons discussed elsewhere, that policy failed with the signature of the Anglo-French Entente in 1904.

Despite the naval policy but, perhaps because of German foreign policy, Britain had compromised with France and begun to reconstruct her security on the basis of an agreement not with Germany, but with France. All that was left for the German naval programme was the choice between abandonment, or a straightforward attempt to outbuild Britain in the course of time. For Germany this was not a real choice, and building went on. In two years, however, the situation changed dramatically, so that another version of Tirpitz's policy could be tried. The cause of this revolution was paradoxically a technologically advanced British invention: HMS *Dreadnought*.

The origins of HMS *Dreadnought*, which gave her name to this class of battleship, were almost all to be found in the thinking of Admiral Sir John Fisher, a seaman of immense ability, unfailing pugnacity and possessed of an unshakeable conviction that his vision was right. He based his ideas on those of the Italian designer, Cuniberti, and aimed to build a ship which could outgun and outsteam any of her rivals. The *Dreadnought*'s advantages were impressive and completely justified Admiral Fisher's faith. She had oil-fired turbines which were more reliable and faster than coal burners; she carried ten twelve-inch guns compared with the normal four twelve-inch guns with which other battleships were equipped. The implications of this deadly ship were frightening. One or two Dreadnoughts were virtually useless when serving with a pre-Dreadnought fleet, because their speed could be satisfactorily deployed tactically only among vessels of their own kind. A fleet of Dreadnoughts, however, could most certainly defeat a pre-Dreadnought fleet three times its own size. If the Dreadnought was to be built, it had to be built in large numbers; and it was the largest fleet – the British – which was, ironically, to suffer most. Britain had invented the Dreadnought and, slipping her through the estimates at the time of the change of government in 1905, Britain built the first example of the type. There was no doubt that Gresham's Law would operate against outdated ships, and Britain depended for her security on her pre-Dreadnought fleet. Certainly she would retain some advantages from her huge existing navy, but the invention of the Dreadnought gave the Germans a chance to outbuild Britain on a more or less equal footing. Once again there was a chance of persuading Britain into an agreement with Germany via the naval question, or of trying straightforwardly to achieve a German superiority at least in local waters.[6]

II

While some of these factors were felt in particular ways, perhaps most clearly demonstrated in the case of the two phases in Anglo-German naval rivalry, other consequences had a general effect. The most obvious of these was the change in the speed and efficiency of communications. In terms of transport, the development or completion of railway systems, long achieved in countries such as Britain, France and Germany, came towards the end of the century to have a profound effect upon the potential – and therefore the potential for creating anxiety – of the great continental powers, Russia and the United States of America. For them could follow the development of what Mackinder called the 'heartlands', and for them could come the advantages of a true development into a unitary state; above all, the new continental railways removed from both states the need to depend on their own or somebody else's sea-power to preserve communication between different parts of their dominions. This constituted a great transfer of power from the coastal societies of the world to new bases in the vast land-masses, hitherto improperly administered and economically underdeveloped.[7] This process was only beginning in the latter part of the nineteenth century, but it had advanced enough to induce in some German minds the notion that German success, or even just German security, could only be achieved by creating a Central European base for the German Empire.

Occurring in parallel, the enormous fillip given to sea transport by the steam engine did something to conceal the importance of the development of more efficient methods of movement on land. The latter part of the nineteenth century produced in both civil and military shipping a great advance in size and in speed. The combination of a greater spread of the ability to build great ships amongst the powers with the greater efficiency of those ships explains much of the concentration upon naval expansion, of which Germany's was only one – if the most serious – example. It may, in a sense, have been the swansong of navalism, but it nonetheless had the plain consequence of bringing the world into much more rapid communication with even its most distant areas, and produced international results of which the Anglo-Japanese Alliance of 1902 was an example.

Another change in the field of communications which was largely common in its effects was the invention and extension of the electric telegraph. If it is farfetched to claim, as has been done, that the Crimean War was started because the telegraph extended only to Vienna in 1854, and had not yet reached Constantinople – where uncontrolled ambassadors created a conflict[8] – it is plain that by the 1870s the spread of the telegraph had produced a new speed and immediacy in international politics. It had the effect of both reducing the remoteness of non-European areas and increasing the authority of foreign ministers and foreign offices, thereby decreasing the flexibility which local discretion had sometimes given. This, perhaps in a small way, contributed to a situation, as in the Far East at the turn of the century, where there was almost no latent conflict which could fail to come within the orbit of the European powers, and yet at the same time be dealt with in a manner reflecting the immediate preoccupations of the home government.

Most of these considerations have related directly to international affairs or to their bases. There are, however, other respects in which international affairs were affected indirectly by the consequences of the later nineteenth century industrial and technological advances. The most striking of these was the change in the nature of the state itself. Throughout the century there had been a continuing tendency for governments to see themselves more and more as ranged with their own societies in contrast to, if not necessarily against, other states. After 1848 the process was accelerated by the growth of a popular nationalism, of which the regime of Napoleon III was as good an example as the nationalist movements in Germany and Italy. All governments, except that of the Habsburg Empire, benefitted from and adjusted to this development, and certainly in the case of Napoleon III their foreign policies were to some extent affected by it. This change of stance was not, however, so important a cause of change in the attitude of governments to their own societies and to others, as was the administrative consequence of the emergence of new industrial societies. It can readily be imagined how the evolution of great urban conurbations, the establishment of great centres of heavy industry, even the appearance of large-scale railway systems, themselves imposed the need as well as the means to embark upon an enormous swelling of the administrative obligations of the government. And perhaps the most impelling of all these factors was the expansion of the population in most European states, though most remarkably in Germany. Had the new pressures on governments come simply from industrial and technological change, they would have been striking; reinforced by a demographic revolution, they were irresistible. Thus there followed a spate of legislation dealing with safety, requiring staff to administer new regulations. Governments, either centrally or locally, found it necessary to take on new responsibilities in relation to housing, water supplies and sewage. With the growth in scope of the governmental machine, the machine itself grew. In Austria–Hungary, where there was in any case a tradition of a centralised bureaucracy, the needs of the modern world turned the civil service itself into a political battleground in which many nationalist tactics could be deployed.

Beginning notably in Germany under Bismarck, controls which mainly affected enterprises or transport in various ways spread slowly but inexorably into demands for social legislation, affecting health and employment. At this point, the expansion of the state became more of a political question than it had earlier been, and served to show how much politics themselves had been changed by the appearance of an industrial proletariat. The first signs of the techniques of mass influence began to show themselves, whether it was in the reorganisation of the structure of political parties – let alone their policies – in the more democratic societies or in the more sinister attempts by German governments to use policies sometimes principally designed to mislead mass opinion in order to protect themselves against the social and suffrage demands of the new Germany. All of these developments, together with the expenditure incurred in keeping up with or joining the general armaments expansion of the period, put governments into severe difficulties in the raising of new revenues. The imposition of heavier and heavier taxation naturally proposed new questions about where it should fall, which in Germany served to aggravate the always sensitive problem of the protected Prussian agrarian classes, and in Britain produced virulent arguments in the early 1900s over the taxation of land. But whatever remedies individual governments adopted they could not avoid the sharpening of political questions, nor the simplification of issues which was such a marked result of the need to woo mass opinion. Nor could they avoid, even if they had wished to, the steady extension of state tentacles into everyday life. The average person found himself powerfully affected by the regulations and taxation of governments, at either state or local level. Government which had earlier been conducted in an informed and leisurely way, and in a clear social context, came to resemble more a scramble for power, achieved by simplistic discussion of mass issues in a fashion suitable for the newly or barely literate to absorb through the organs of the popular press. And when men acquired the power they sought, they found it to be so great that it was beyond their control. The sheer quantity of business had led to large-scale delegation, and with it to the steady increase of delegated authority.

These kinds of development led to a quickening of the process which the success of the doctrines of nationalism had begun, and brought at the moment of its apparent greatest sovereignty an almost complete identification of government and society within states. With it came great difficulties and complexities in the processes of government, whether administrative or political, which reduced the flexibility and breadth of view of Cabinets.[9]

Some consequences of this can be seen soon after 1870. When Bismarck was constructing his web of agreements after 1878, he was assisted in re-establishing the principles of the Concert by using methods which had hitherto been confined to periods of war of the *ancien régime*. These succeeded because although governments were extremely reluctant to commit themselves, they were impelled to do so. The consequence of this uncomfortable contradiction was that after 1878 there appeared the network of defensive agreements which was so characteristic of Bismarck's period. These agreements were entered into only with difficulty; they were widely publicised; they were short-term; and each renewal tended to bring out the reluctance of governments rather than to strengthen their resolve. It was also most noticeably the case that these agreements could be, and often were, made in apparently incompatible directions: any power was as likely to be restrained by its ally as its opponent. But if these agreements were precise, short-term, defensive and apparently insufficiently binding to inhibit the making of contradictory alliances, why were they made at all? The clue is to be found in observing that the restrictions that reluctant powers carefully wrote into their agreements were designed to preserve their freedom of action. They felt their independence to be threatened, and yet felt the need to assert it. The plain facts of the international situation forbade to European states the isolation that Britain could mostly enjoy. Indeed, the Concert had depended to some extent upon the willingness of states to surrender a modicum of sovereignty for the sake of customary restraint, and upon the readiness of states to come to conferences. But after 1878, states began to seek for ways of buttressing their independence and ceased to be prepared to come to conferences. To force an unwilling government to a conference came to be regarded as an indication of its defeat.[10]

The development of the armaments deadlock increased the touchiness of governments already so predisposed by the changes, previously noted, in the character of the state. The insistence of states on the preservation of their freedom of action was expressed as much by their armed preparedness as by their diplomatic incompatibility. Technological advances joined with administrative improvements not only to change the nature of the state, but also to change the standing of the armed forces. Germany's example, in creating an army which was always ready for a rapid mobilisation and relied upon conscription to maintain its large numbers, was followed in other European states. Again, the attempt to secure independence produced the opposite result. For technological improvements pushed weapon development far ahead of mobility and in so doing imposed tactical inflexibility. The deadlock produced an ever-increasing emphasis upon weight and numbers, which alone could bring victory to the attacking party. Military expenditure became crippling, both in the sheer quantity of men and materials being maintained and in the quality of research which was being done to ensure that no possible improvement in technique was missed. These costs were incurred at a time when the responsibilities of the state in the social field were also increasing expensively and contributed to a tactical and psychological desire for alliances. Nothing is more illustrative of the acute problem which states were encountering in this sphere than the very precise provisions contained in the alliances for military aid. In the case of the Franco-Russian Alliance, the whole agreement really rested upon a military commitment, which the two powers had little intention of carrying into the diplomatic field.[11]

Another paradoxical feature of the last years of the nineteenth century was a further consequence of the factors which contributed to the development of the modern state. The administrative concerns to which governments were forced to pay attention also appeared on the international scene, and one of the effects of internal regulation of these problems was the realisation that in many cases governments had come to desire a measure of international control. In areas such as postage, telegraphs and disease, states exhibited a willingness to co-operate and produced a flood of international legislation which has found its apotheosis in the non-political organs of the United Nations. The extent of the co-operation was impressive and misleading. It was another aspect of the same developments which were making states less and not more willing to take combined action in the political sphere: the very closeness of the relationship between states in some matters only served to increase their self-consciousness over the vital issues. Nevertheless, the hopes which administrative co-operation raised began to take more concrete form when increasing tension indicated the need to substitute a new international system for the old Concert. Already the need to deal with parts of the world which had not hitherto formed a usual part of the framework of international politics had added strength to the case for the establishment of a binding code of international law. Moreover, the increasing use of bilateral treaties of arbitration, by which specified issues were agreed to be subject to arbitration if disagreement arose, seemed to point a way forward. Significantly the proposal for such a system of compulsory arbitration started from an assumption that the

existence of states was an irreversible fact, where before such program-
mes had sought to limit the effectiveness of states in quasi-federal
schemes, like the Congress system.[12]

The Tsar of Russia, perhaps because his was the first state to
be seriously affected by expenditure on armaments, called an international peace conference which met at The Hague in 1898. It was a failure,
as might have been expected; but a failure which neatly represented the
dilemma in which states found themselves. They agreed readily on the
improvement and codification of the rules of warfare; they agreed that
any government might offer to mediate in a dispute without risk of
opprobrium – no doubt in the hope that others might be willing to
restrain their allies for them; and they established what was in fact a
weakly constituted *ad hoc* international commission, but grandly called a
Court of International Arbitration. 'Not a single power', wrote the
American delegate, 'was willing to bring itself to submit all questions to
arbitration, and least of all the United States. A few nations were willing
to accept it in minor matters – as for example postal or monetary
difficulties and the like.'[13] The substitution of a legal system of
international relations for the customary looser political system hitherto
employed was never likely to be successful (as the history of the League
of Nations was to show); but states were in no way prepared to try in
1898. The development of the modern state had reached the adolescent
stage, where the adult version was more visible than the child; they were
potent yet uncertain of their powers; aggressively individual yet afraid.
They were uncomfortable within themselves, and communicated discomfort to their friends and neighbours.

Nor was this development without effect on the conduct of policy, as
well as its objectives. Foreign policies were very far from being
conducted according to popular desires – indeed the charge has often
been laid that the war of 1914 would never have come about if they had
been more subject to popular control. Nevertheless, in a limited way
there was a change in this direction. The consciousness of individuality
which the late nineteenth century gave to the nation-state had the effect of
finally ending that unwritten alliance between government and government which was the result of their fear of revolution, and of the social
similarity of their members. Governments now began to see themselves as
more closely related to their own peoples and if popular desires did not
formulate foreign policy, it was no longer wise for governments to neglect
propaganda in favour of the policies they had adopted. This is the age, for
example, when the state visit became something more than the family or

social occasion it had tended to be in the past. The Anglo-French *Entente* of 1904 was publicly initiated by Edward VII's state visit to Paris and cemented by President Loubet's return fixture. French public opinion had to be introduced to the *Entente* gently and Edward, when in Paris, materially affected it – sometimes, it is said, by blowing kisses to celebrated courtesans across the theatre. The growth of mass opinion did not form foreign policy, but it had to be taken into account if its direction was to be altered.

Further Reading

G. Barraclough, *An Introduction to Contemporary History* (Pelican, 1967).

J. H. Clapham, *The Economic Development of France and Germany* (Cambridge: CUP, 1945).

F. H. Hinsley, *Power and the Pursuit of Peace* (Cambridge: CUP, 1963).

E. J. Hobsbawm, *Industry and Empire* (Weidenfeld and Nicolson, 1968).

P. M. Kennedy, *The Rise and Fall of British Naval Mastery* (Allen Lane, 1976).

P. Mathias, *The First Industrial Nation* (Methuen, 1969).

E. L. Woodward, *Great Britain and the German Navy* (Oxford: OUP, 1935).

PART TWO

The Response to Insecurity

5. The Grouping of Powers, 1890–1907

I

From 1890 it was extremely likely, if not certain, that the effects of the factors discussed in the preceding chapters would begin to create a sense of insecurity within the international system, first and most obviously because of the change in the distribution of power brought about by the rise of Germany. Indeed such a change might have been sensed before 1890. To start with, however, it was not apparent. Bismarck was always more aware of Germany's weakness than of her strength, so much so that it apparently troubled his sleep. This weakness was primarily strategic. Germany lay in the middle of Europe, wide open to the possibility of war on two fronts; she was condemned to bad relations with her western neighbour until, if ever, the results of the Franco-Prussian War of 1870 were forgotten; her two eastern neighbours were, for traditional reasons of clashing Balkan interests, at semi-permanent loggerheads. Germany herself was bound for some years to be regarded with suspicion as an unknown quantity and, when that quantity was known, to suffer the disadvantages of possessing very great power.

Bismarck's policy was quiescent, supine in the pursuit of any German interest other than that of peace. He at first attempted a universal eastern combination of the old dynastic kind – the Three Emperors' League – which might be expected to serve the twin purposes of keeping France isolated and the Balkans at peace. The crisis in the Near East of 1876–8 put an end to this perhaps sanguine scheme and forced Bismarck to make a choice between Russia and Austria. Nevertheless, after the Austro-German Alliance of 1879, Bismarck continued to keep Russia in play, hoping to nullify the effect of his choice by means of renewable 'insurance' treaties with Russia. Russo-German friendship, if in any serious crisis it would now have to be abandoned, must be maintained as long as possible to prevent any Franco-Russian *rapprochement*.

Continuously Bismarck sought to keep the status quo, whether it meant admitting Italy to the Dual Alliance in 1882 – for the sake of preserving Italo-Austrian peace and to keep her out of the hands of France – or venturing into the colonial race in Africa, in order to appease France on the one hand and convince Britain of the merits of German friendship on the other. All the complications of his policies were designed to secure international immobility, and its cardinal feature was restraint – a restraint which was extended to Austria, for whom there was as yet no blank cheque in the Balkans. When he was dismissed, the British *Spectator* was not alone in thinking that the great flywheel which governed European politics had been withdrawn and viewing such an event with justifiable alarm.[1]

In Germany itself, however, there were some with few, if any, regrets for the Chancellor's passing. They were impressed not so much with the success and safety which Bismarck's policies had brought, but with the power and greatness which had come to Germany during his period of office. If Bismarck's successors were to lead Germany to disaster, it was not so much because he had laid up for them an impossible political heritage, or because his policies were too complex for lesser men to follow: it was because they rejected them as unnecessarily cautious and inadequate to Germany's status. But as Germany grew, as she did after 1895, to be more powerful than any European combination, and as the international system was subjected to increasing pressures, it was more than ever dangerous for Germany to expose herself to the possibility of encirclement.

Almost immediately the exponents of what was called the 'New Course' in foreign affairs omitted to renew the insurance treaty with Russia and her slow *rapprochement* with France began. Moreover, it was not long before, at least from a military standpoint, Berlin removed the restraining hand from Austria's shoulder. In general terms, powers already grappling with the manifold problems which faced the modern state began to find that underlying assumptions about the conduct of international affairs in Europe no longer held good, and were challenged by new voices from Berlin. The parity of power had gone, and was seen to be gone.

It became clear soon after William II's accession in 1888 that Bismarck was going to have considerable difficulty in having the Reinsurance Treaty with Russia renewed. The new Emperor was persuaded by military men such as Field Marshal von Waldersee that planning must be done in case of a war on two fronts, and this meant co-operation with

Austria–Hungary in Galicia. War on two fronts also meant that Germany must seek the friendship of Britain – even if in William's eyes it was not already desirable as a liberal gesture. From 1888 until 1890 Anglo-German relations were more cordial than at any time, as the Triple Alliance sought to gain Britain's adhesion. The treaty exchanging Heligoland for Zanzibar marked the zenith of this process, but without marking Britain's entry into the 1882 agreement.[2]

In 1889, William told Francis Joseph that whatever the reason for it, Austrian mobilisation would be followed by German mobilisation on the next day. Tsar Alexander III, visiting Berlin in October 1889, was unable to be cordial with anyone save the French ambassador. He was moved no doubt by the fact that late in the previous year, a Russian loan had been floated on the Paris *Bourse*, and the French had supplied Russia with Lebel rifles, demanding only a promise that they would not be used against France. William proceeded in November 1888 to visit Constantinople, which was hardly a gesture calculated to keep the Russians away from Paris. Meanwhile, the conflict with Bismarck ended in his dismissal, and when Shuvalov, the Russian ambassador in Berlin, proposed the renewal of the Reinsurance Treaty in March 1890, he was told that the Treaty would not be continued, although German policy would remain unaltered. Giers, the Russian Foreign Minister, tried to obtain even a watered-down version of the treaty, but still the Germans would not renew. They were by now concerned to secure British co-operation in their wholehearted support of Austria–Hungary. The New Course was intended to simplify German policy, despite the complexity of the international situation, and it was thought that Britain could be gained for the Triple Alliance, and thus ensure the safety of the Near East without the need to balance between Austria and Russia. Certainly they would do nothing that might upset British sensibilities in regard to Russia. Nor was Caprivi unconscious of the effect which would be produced if the Kaiser succeeded in building the large navy that he was already agitating for: 'There must be a battle', wrote Caprivi, 'and the great war, which hangs over Germany's head, must be fought before we can build as many ships as Germany and the Emperor . . . want.'[3] While that operation was carried through, Britain must be kept at least in play. The Heligoland treaty followed in July 1890, while the French and the Russians both tried to mend their fences with Britain and Germany respectively. They both failed, and the arrest of fourteen Russian nihilists in their traditional Parisian hideout took on a new significance. Boisdeffre, the French chief of staff, visited St Petersburg in August but with no result; and in the face of Italian manoeuvres which seemed to suggest a coalition to drive France out of Tunis, the French put pressure on Russia. They prevented the flotation of a second Russian loan in Paris, when the Russians were in the direst financial straits, and secured the first real change of policy. Alexander III had also been irritated by British co-operation with the Triple Alliance, and when the Russians said that they were now interested in a military convention, a French squadron visited the Russian naval base at Kronstadt in July 1891. Negotiations of a reluctant kind ensued, but when the French squadron was invited to visit Portsmouth on its return the possibility of an Anglo-French agreement, distant though it was, caused Alexander III to agree to a political *entente* which was finalised in August.

This was an anti-British arrangement at bottom – as the Franco-Russian Alliance was to remain until the Germans made it otherwise – but the French also wanted some security against Germany on their eastern frontier. The two countries could satisfy their requirements only if there was both a political and a military agreement. The political would satisfy the Russians in their conflict with Britain and Asia; the military would satisfy the French, whose geographical position imposed an anti-German bias. Both countries hoped that the agreement would enable them to return to older and more comfortable friendships: with conservative Germany in the case of Russia, with liberal Britain in the case of France.[4]

The French secured a military alliance in August 1892, although it was not confirmed by the Tsar until 1894, by which they were promised support even if they were at war only with Germany; while the Russians obtained the promise that if Austria mobilised against Russia by herself, France would follow suit. No sooner had this convention been agreed than the French, unbeknown to them, were vindicated. For the Germans abandoned the old plans of Moltke, which envisaged attacking Russia first as the most formidable of Germany's enemies, in favour of General Schlieffen's plan for swiftly knocking out France before engaging in a long-drawn-out campaign in Russia. The Schlieffen plan was a perfectly rational military proposition but, in combination with a Franco-Russian alliance, it made encirclement a fact rather than a fear. When it was altered later so as to shift the German attack from the Vosges to Belgium, even the possible neutrality of Britain was thrown away. The consequence of Germany's change of strategy was the need to obtain new and larger army estimates. Caprivi pushed the bill through by emphasising the danger from Russia – which Bismarck would never have done without first securing himself with France – and in so doing attracted the support both of Poles and Radicals.[5]

The Panama scandal in France, which rocked the Third Republic, was the chief cause of the Tsar's delay in approving the convention of August 1892. It even brought about faint suggestions of a Russo-German *rapprochement*; but the support which Caprivi's Army Bill gained in July 1893 soon combined with the passing of the scandal to bring Alexander to a decision. In the end, he seems to have felt that the commitment to France in the West would not be dangerous, because the French were not planning a war of revenge. It was therefore safe to approve the convention which became on 4 January 1894 the Franco-Russian Alliance. It was, Taylor has written,

> A turning point in the history of Europe. With all its reserves and contradictions it was yet a declaration that Russia and France intended to avoid the dependence on Germany into which Austria–Hungary had fallen. Both made a sacrifice of their principles and traditions. The autocrat of all the Russias stood to attention for the Marseillaise; and that hymn of revolutionary nationalism was played in honour of the oppressor of the Poles.[6]

The effect of the Franco-Russian Alliance was not immediately to divide Europe into two camps. Both parties intended different consequences to flow from it, and neither was prepared to compromise its primary political interests in order to please the other. Neither the Triple Alliance, in which after her defeat in Abyssinia Italy became an ever-more doubtful quantity, nor the new combination was as yet of much different character from the other agreements made since 1870; nevertheless, the possibility of rigid divisions was now there, and Bismarck had thought it desirable to devote an enormous amount of time and skill to the creation of an international system which would prevent just such a development.

So long as Russia was primarily concerned with Asiatic affairs, the Dual Alliance could have little European significance. For the Germans the completion of the Trans-Siberian Railway, and Russia's consequent readiness to transfer her ambitions for Constantinople to Peking, was crucial. The consequent agreement between Russia and Austria in 1897 removed the Balkans from the field of conflict. Until the Russian agreement with Britain in 1907 signified that the effect of defeat in 1905 would bring Russia back to the Balkans, the Germans were safe and could continue to assume that Britain must remain at loggerheads with both

France and Russia. Furthermore, this assumption was reinforced by the fact that since the operation of the Franco-Russian Alliance was confined to Asia, it was bound to be obviously anti-British. So much so that Britain could not use her position as virtually a powerful third grouping to balance between the two European combinations. She was driven, in fact, to lean towards the Triple Alliance and, more important, she was driven into difficulties. The Franco-Russian combination, which often appeared to be on the verge of squeezing Britain out of her central position of influence in China, was unlikely to be opposed by Germany. Her immediate interest was to encourage the Asiatic adventures of Paris and St Petersburg, when she did not feel the inclination to join in herself.

Although the Triple Alliance was strengthened militarily at this time, and the restraint which Bismarck had imposed upon Austria was to some extent relaxed, and although France and Russia had formed a reluctant alliance, it was now Britain who was the significant character on the international stage. If there is any continuity to be found in the complexities of international politics in the 1890s it is in the position and policy of Britain. In the first stages this was because, far from divided camps, the chief feature seemed to be an informal continental league against Britain. After 1898, it began to be a question whether she would join one of the existing combinations, with all the momentous consequences that would follow whenever the scene of international conflicts should return to Europe.

By the 1890s Britain had become very aware of her 'isolation': the situation in South Africa, the Venezuela episode[7] and the Far East all made the position clear. Isolation was held to be a traditional policy and for a while, with vociferous aid from Canada,[8] to be a good and necessary policy. It was thought that Britain's constitutional arrangements precluded her from giving pledges to any other power which would be of serious use – at least in peacetime. Salisbury never tired of telling ambassadors how impossible it would be for him to commit Britain to a *casus foederis*, since whether the pledge was honoured or not would depend upon the state of British public opinion at the time, as well as the character of the incident concerned.[9]

That there was some justice in these claims is apparent from the British government's behaviour in August 1914; that they in no way precluded her from giving guarantees is equally clear from the ones that were still in force throughout the period of 'splendid isolation', and the ones she was prepared to give to Portugal and to Japan in 1899 and 1902.[10] In effect, British policy had been left behind by events. Her splendid isolation was not really different from the peacetime policy she had pursued since 1815, nor from the policies of other powers. In the period of Concert, entangling alliances were neither desirable nor necessary; but between 1879 and 1894, the other great powers changed their policies and entered into alliances of a new character, in a search for security which the system was no longer able to give. Britain did not change her policy; indeed, under Mr Gladstone she attempted to revive the Concert in its most binding form.[11] When, therefore, she appeared to suffer disadvantages from the isolated position she had come to be in, it was naturally a matter for comment. Comment quickly turned isolation into splendid isolation and more correctly described it, at least in a loose sense, as having been a traditional policy for which good constitutional reasons could be adduced. It was no longer, however, a safe policy, and under both Rosebery and Salisbury Britain tried to get agreement with Germany and Russia.

The first attempts of Rosebery were wholly unsuccessful. He attempted in 1894 to push the Austrians into recommending an agreement with Britain at Berlin. He promised to fight for the Straits, if France were safely checked – which could only be achieved by Germany. But Caprivi would not now play the game: an Anglo-Austrian agreement was what Germany had always wanted, but an Anglo-German agreement carried too much risk of war with Russia. Seeking to lose none of the advantage that Rosebery's approach had given them, the Germans then tried to bring about an Anglo-Austrian agreement by threatening Rosebery over a treaty that had just been made with the Congo Free State. The intention was to cut the French off from the Upper Nile and it soon proved that, when the Germans regretted their action and withdrew, the French could quite satisfactorily ruin the agreement on their own. A renewed discussion about Egypt followed and, as reliably as usual, failed. The French had still not got the means to make Britain compensate them, even a little, for the occupation and in November 1894 Colonel Marchand's expedition set out to trek across Africa until it arrived on the Upper Nile. This, it was hoped, might bring Britain to genuine negotiations.

With Russia, Rosebery succeeded in making a convention about the Pamir frontier in the autumn of 1894, and was presented soon after with the opportunity to co-operate with the Franco-Russian Alliance in putting pressure on the Turks to cease the massacres of Armenians – massacres which were currently shocking British public opinion. But nothing further came of these feelers: as yet the Russians did not need British assistance anywhere – the Trans-Siberian Railway had seen to that. The

Armenian massacres, however, continuing as they did until 1896, provided Salisbury, who returned to office in 1895, with a new opportunity to approach Russia. Exactly what Lord Salisbury was trying to achieve in the summer of 1895 has been the subject of some discussion.[12] He was in the process of changing his mind about the eastern question, and nothing that occurred during the appalling massacres of Armenians slowed up the process. It was clear that, as he had come to suspect in 1878–9, there was really no hope for Turkey. The Ottoman empire could be persuaded into none of the reforms which might restore its strength and put a stop to the inhumane scandals that periodically rocked the conscience of civilised society. What was done at the Congress of Berlin, coupled with the British hold on Egypt, seemed to render the route to India quite as secure as it could be made with or without a paramount influence at the Straits. Perhaps the time had come to reverse Lord Palmerston's policy and begin the partition of Turkey. It was to be another two years before Salisbury could bring himself to change his mind officially and inform the Austrians that Britain no longer held to the policy which they had pursued in common for so long. When he did so, the result was to make Vienna all the more ready to agree with Russia in 1897 to a mutual self-denying ordinance in the Balkans. For the moment, however, the British Prime Minister indulged in some kite-flying that was very typical of his habit of confiding in foreign representatives in a speculative way. His daughter reported that he would have much 'resented having his words quoted as evidence', when he made such informal suggestions.[13]

There is no doubt, however, that he wanted to come to an agreement with Russia if he could, and he approached her with that in mind, as he was to do again in 1898. In his famous conversation with the German ambassador, in whom he had confidence, he was also testing the effect that British conversion to partition would have upon the Germans and perhaps, by a leakage to St Petersburg, hoping that it might encourage the Russians to move in his direction. Certainly he regretted that the chance of partition was lost in 1853; that Britain had 'backed the wrong horse'; and contemplated the idea of letting the Russians have Constantinople, with all that would follow from such a momentous change. He also knew that the Admiralty no longer thought it possible to force the Straits, and that the Services were generally doubtful about its strategic value. Nevertheless, the offer was never made to the Russians directly until during the First World War, and was generally reserved as a hint to be dropped occasionally to Russia. It was used in this way in 1906.[14] In 1895 the German government thought that the whole affair was an attempt to wean Russia from her and inaugurate an Anglo-Russian *rapprochement*, which Salisbury would have liked; but Hatzfeldt, the ambassador in London, thought that Salisbury was genuinely proposing an internationally agreed partition – for which, of course the co-operation of the Triple Alliance would have been required, and hence the conversation. They were not incompatible aims, unless the Germans made them so, and their suspicions brought both propositions to nothing.

In 1898, Salisbury tried again to win the Russians for an agreement which would cover both China and Turkey. There were some signs that the German seizure of Kiaochow had caused the Russians to consider an agreement with Britain in China. What they wanted, however, was a straight partition of China, leaving to the beneficiaries a completely free hand in their respective areas. What Salisbury offered was 'no partition of territory, but only a partition of preponderance', together with 'no infraction of existing rights'. The Russians put some purely Chinese proposals, which were then dropped when it became known that the Peking government had secured a loan from the British-owned Hong Kong and Shanghai Bank. The Russians proceeded soon afterwards to show contempt for the whole proposition by forcing the Chinese to surrender Port Arthur.[15]

The failure of Salisbury's negotiations with Russia in 1898 and her subsequent seizure of Port Arthur seemed to be the signal for the 'scramble for China' to begin. Britain took Weihaiwei and again tried to find allies. Salisbury continued to believe that isolation would serve Britain quite well; but his vigorous and commercially minded colleague, Chamberlain, was intent on gaining an ally. However uncomfortable the situation was, either in China or in South Africa, Salisbury was probably right. The naval expansion that had been undertaken since 1889 rendered Britain genuinely independent, until such time as she should be seriously challenged by Germany – which did not occur until 1901 – or faced with an attempt by one power at continental domination, and she did not really suspect that until 1906. Chamberlain would not be gainsaid, however, and Salisbury would no doubt have been perfectly content, had he been successful, to be handling a less unpleasant situation. Secret negotiations followed, and so did the celebrated series of public speeches with which Chamberlain tried to woo the Germans. The high point of the first set of Anglo-German exchanges came when Hatzfeldt – the German ambassador in London – gave Bülow's proposals to Chamberlain on 1 April 1898. They envisaged a public agreement, but one which was clearly intended to isolate the French. Chamberlain returned to the subject of China: he too wanted a public agreement, he said, but Russia must be prevented from advancing further in China.

> I said that if we had a clear understanding with Germany and a joint policy we might adopt a much stronger policy than if we were alone, and in this case we could lay down the bases of a settlement in China which neither France nor Russia would be likely to resist... I said that speaking for myself only, that I thought we might say to Russia – 'You have got all you say you want. We are ready to recognise your position, but you must go no further. The rest of China is under our joint protection.'[16]

The Germans were understandably doubtful about an arrangement which appeared to make them into a buffer between Britain and Russia and, moreover, allowed the British to walk off with the most fruitful proposition in China – the Yangtse Basin. Nevertheless, Balfour actually went as far as to sound the House of Commons indirectly about the possibility of an Anglo-German alliance in China.

The German attitude was compounded of two elements: they would not go further with schemes which did nothing to relieve their continental position, or which threatened good relations with Russia; but equally they were sure that by keeping Britain in play she could eventually be brought to make the agreement that Germany required, out of desperation. The Kaiser, for one, had never forgotten the occasion in 1893 when during a crisis over Siam,[17] in which the British had suddenly feared war with France, he had been in receipt of urgent appeals for help from Rosebery. There was in fact neither real danger of war nor need for help, but the Germans began to think then, and became ever more sure, that if they waited for long enough they could have an alliance with Britain on their own terms. Until that time, as Bülow wrote, 'we must remain independent between the two powers (Britain and Russia); we must be the tongue of the balance, not the restlessly swinging pendulum.'[18]

As this attitude percolated back to London, Chamberlain said to Hatzfeldt that he gathered that his suggestions had been premature, and reminded him 'of the French proverb *le bonheur qui passe*'.[19] Salisbury shortly afterwards commented that it was evidently Hatzfeldt's business 'to pour cold water'. Having made a speech at the Albert Hall – the 'Dying Nations' speech – in which it was clear that Salisbury took the Far-Eastern situation less seriously than Chamberlain, he told Hatzfeldt a few days later quite bluntly: 'You ask too much for our friendship.'[20] Chamberlain turned to the United States. In Birmingham he addressed the Unionist Association: 'I even go so far as to say that, terrible as war may be, even war itself would be cheaply purchased if in a great and noble cause the Stars and Stripes and the Union Jack should wave together over an Anglo-Saxon alliance.'[21] The reaction in the United States was unfavourable, despite the growing American conviction that Germany was a new enemy in the Pacific. 'There is', wrote Ambassador John Hay, 'in the German mind something monstrous in the thought that a war should take place anywhere and they not profit by it.'[22]

Despite the disagreement over the American occupation of the Philippines and continued bickering in China, Anglo-German relations remained basically good, if only because Britain was to be kept in play and because Germany had need of British goodwill outside Europe. She found a way of achieving these ends through the outbreak of serious conflict with the Boers. If the Suez Canal was now thought to be a British interest and sufficiently under British control to warrant giving up the Straits, the Cape was yet more vital: communications to India and the Far East could always go by that route if necessary. However reliable Suez might seem to be, the Cape had to be even more secure. Thus Britain found herself fast approaching a war with the Boer republics which seemed to threaten that security. The first German reaction was to try once again to raise a continental league against Britain, a proposition which failed miserably. They then decided to be Britain's only friend in the face of the most extreme hostility she faced at any time between 1815 and 1914. Later on, in the famous *Daily Telegraph* interview of 1908, the Kaiser was to claim that he alone stood between the anger of the German people and Britain, and that he had prevented the intervention of France and Russia against her while the war was in progress. Whether this was true or not, German assistance to Britain was not disinterested, for she hoped that the moment of British surrender to her terms for an alliance had arrived; nor without price, since the one concrete agreement to emerge from three years of desultory negotiation was the Anglo-German division of the Portuguese colonies.

This agreement followed from the need of the British government to shut the Boers off from the sea, and thus defeat the Transvaal without a war. The only way to achieve this was to persuade the Portuguese government to close the railway to Delegoa Bay on the coast of the Portuguese colony of Mozambique. The most effective weapon which the British government had to bring the Portuguese to their way of thinking was financial. In 1897 Portugal was not only nearly bankrupt, but also faced with revolution. The dynasty was collapsing and the republican insurgents were making it increasingly difficult to govern metropolitan Portugal, let alone the colonies. In addition to these difficulties, there was no doubt that Portugal was soon going to be faced with an unfavourable judgement from an arbitration tribunal sitting at Berne. The Portuguese government had seized the Mozambique Railway and shareholders were pressing for compensation. When the 'Berne' award came there would be no funds with which to pay it. A danger arose that Germany, who had long-standing ambitions in Mozambique, might seize the opportunity to insert herself unless the British took prompt action. Despite their situation the Portuguese government were not anxious to make an agreement in which British intentions in the matter of the railway were as suspect as the German reaction might be violent. Not even the threat of naval action would move them, and negotiations for a loan in exchange for assurances about the use of the railway were dropped.

Events soon taught the Portuguese from whom they had most to fear. The Germans seized Kiaochow in November 1897, and in doing so alarmed all the smaller European colonial empires. Portugal changed her mind and agreed to settle with British in return for money and a reaffirmation of the ancient Portuguese alliance. At this point, the German government got wind of what was afoot, and Hatzfeldt openly threatened Salisbury with the formation of a continental league if the Germans were not admitted to any arrangements entered into with Portugal. Their own possessions gave them an interest in the area, and their hopes of benefiting from what appeared to be the certain collapse of Portugal gave them a sense of urgency. The result was an agreement, concluded in August 1898, which carefully carved up the Portuguese colonies of Angola and Mozambique by tying up the various portions that each power would inherit as security for the corresponding half of the anticipated joint loan. The agreement never came into force, as there never was a joint loan, and served in the first instance merely to exacerbate Anglo-German relations, and latterly to become the source of an unsuccessful means of improving them by the revisions of 1913–14. The Germans soon came to suspect quite rightly that the exigencies of the Boer War had caused the British to give binding pledges to Portugal on the integrity of her empire, while doing all she could to avoid having to face the consequences of her contradictory agreement with Germany. The Germans always supposed that the demise of the Portuguese Empire was to be assisted by the 1898 Convention; but the agreement expressed the opposite sentiments, which the British repeated verbally. They regarded it as a long-stop affair, to be put into operation if all other remedial measures failed. The German Foreign Secretary wrote in 1913: 'The general feeling in Germany is that in 1898 we were duped by England and done out of the price for which we stipulated in return for our attitude towards England in the Boer War.'[23]

In 1899 there came another attempt on the part of Chamberlain to get an Anglo-German agreement. The Kaiser and Bülow came to London at the height of anti-British feeling on the continent, and although they had no intention of concluding any alliance – unless, of course they were offered a European agreement – Chamberlain seized the moment to make a famous speech. There should be, he said, 'a new triple alliance between the Teutonic race and the two great branches of the Anglo-Saxon race . . . The natural alliance is between ourselves and the great German empire.'[24] Two months later, however, British ships stopped and searched some German mail-boats in South African waters with the result that, during the ensuing anti-British outcry, the necessary support was readily found for a new German Navy Law. Nor was the position helped when, after the Boxer Rising of 1900, the Russians were so clearly the gainers that an Anglo-German agreement upholding the doctrine of the 'open door' was made and then as quickly deserted by the Germans.

This should have been the end of these *pourparlers*, but for the operations of Baron Eckhardstein of the German Embassy in London and the worsening crisis in China. The Far East contributed to a continuing desire on the part of both Britain and Germany for an agreement, and the Baron, left in charge of the Embassy during a serious illness of Hatzfeldt, allowed his British sympathies to create a situation in which both parties thought that the initiative had come from the other. The Germans began to think that the British were coming to them at last, and Lansdowne, the new British Foreign Secretary, thought that it would be possible to make the arrangement that Britain had always wanted, whereby she would receive support from the Triple Alliance without actually joining it. The result was never in doubt, but the attempt has achieved much notice because it produced both the only formal draft alliance prepared by the Foreign Office, and Salisbury's classic memorandum of 29 May 1901: 'Count Hatzfeldt speaks of our "isolation" as constituting a serious danger for us. *Have we ever felt that danger practically?* It would hardly be wise to incur novel and most onerous obligations, in order to guard against *a danger in whose existence we have no historical reason for believing*. Furthermore, the demands of a democratic state in the conduct of foreign policy made a weightier objection. 'The fatal circumstance is that *neither we nor the Germans are competent to make the suggested promises*.'[25]

Much discussion has taken place about the 'lost opportunity' of 1898–1901, particularly by historians participating in the great debate about the causes of the First World War, which was precipitated by the guilt clauses in the Versailles Treaty. A great chance to avert an Anglo-German war was apparently thrown away: by the Germans who held out for too long and for too much, or by Salisbury who did not appreciate the true gravity of the situation and was blinded by his dislike of the Kaiser. Quite soon after the war, however, more mature consideration led the great German historian Gerhard Ritter to doubt whether the opportunity was real, and both Langer and Taylor have agreed with him in later studies. It is certainly observable that, as Langer emphasises, Britain tried for an agreement with Russia as often as she tried Germany. It is clear that what was desired was an agreement with somebody: preferably Russia with whom there existed an obvious quarrel, failing that Germany, and/or the United States, and finally with Japan. It is equally true, as has been widely noticed, that there was neither common ground nor common dispute between Britain and Germany. Their objectives were markedly different in the context of current international politics. The international situation in 1900 had some of the same characteristics as when Bismarck had thought it desirable to do no more than keep Britain agreeable for most of the time while concentrating on the safety of his continental system.[26]

This was the rub: Bismarck would never have fought Russia for the sake of British India; Bülow, too, refused to 'pull Britain's chestnuts out of the fire'. German interests were primarily European interests and demanded security on two frontiers. British interests were worldwide, particularly Asiatic, and demanded security against Russia or a continental league. The continental league occasionally cast a shadow, but could never have been a reality in the face of the refurbished British fleet, even if continental conditions had given it much more hope, which they did not. Against Russia, only Japan was a possible ally, and she expended great efforts to agree with St Petersburg and avoid conflict. The United States, it is true, was beginning to reverse her traditional policy, showing friendship towards Britain and hostility towards Russia; but this was a combination that was for 1949 rather than 1899.

Nevertheless, the Far East with its foretaste of genuine world politics, does suggest other considerations. If it is perfectly true that German interests were such that they could not seriously be served by anything short of a British declaration of neutrality in Europe, not all Germans were by any means intent upon the safety of their European position. The successors of Bismarck were impressed not so much with Germany's weakness, but with her enormous strength. The increase of German power in the 1890s made her not only the equal of any one European power, but also stronger than any combination; and her obvious dominance was unlikely to bring back a more realistic conception of her wisest policy. The appearance of a High Seas fleet, the ever-more frequent out-croppings of *Weltpolitik*, the steady relaxation of control over Austria–Hungary, arising in part from a loss of stability within German society and government, all argued a new attitude towards international politics which was of the very gravest consequence.

In terms of sheer reality, the German Empire could not be a world power, despite its great weight, principally because, unlike Britain, its home base was not secure. This was primarily why no agreement with Britain was possible. But the fact that the Germans desired to be a world power, and not only believed themselves thwarted by Britain, but also appreciated that in the nature of things Russia and the United States were destined to be world powers, gave rise to a different sort of policy. The Far East had shown this more clearly than at any time since de Tocqueville had forecast it earlier in the century. For until the 1890s, the rise of Germany had brought with it such a reawakening of European power and activity that the real trends of the future had been obscured. Thus while Germany pursued a false world policy, more as a sop to internal malcontents than anything else, she prepared to make herself into a genuine contender for world-power status, able to stand beside Britain, Russia and the United States.

It is this consideration which puts the negotiations of 1898–1901 in a different light. It was foolish of Germany to hold out for better terms with Britain when what she wanted, as Tirpitz's original plan had envisaged, was an agreement which would help to hold the ring while Europe was overcome. Germany could only have world power on the basis of hegemony in Europe, and no other considerations should have weighed against improving the chance of a successful outcome for this vital operation. Had Germany been prepared to achieve world power in two stages, then it was quite comprehensible that she should have behaved as she did in 1901. But by rejecting an agreement with Britain, and by pursuing needlessly violent policies all round the world, Germany made certain that she would have to take on Britain as part of her bid for European hegemony. There was a chance of avoiding such a conflict, and this was the opportunity that was lost.

Germans assumed that Britain was their enemy because of her world-power status and yet believed that she was decadent, on the road to bankruptcy induced by the naval race, or would fail in the last resort to find the courage to go to war. It was in a way symptomatic of the German muddle that some of her leaders – industrialists like Ballin, politicians like Bethmann-Hollweg – sought constantly to secure Britain's neutrality, while her military men planned always on the assumption that Britain would be their enemy, and indeed wove plans which ensured that she must be.

Thus, it is clear that if the Germans were on one level wholly justified in not making an agreement with Britain between 1898 and 1901, it was nevertheless an error in the long run. The chain of events which led from the formation of the Anglo-Japanese Alliance in 1902, first to the *Entente* of 1904 and secondly, after the consequent Russo-Japanese War, to the Anglo-Russian convention of 1907, brought about the final encirclement of Germany. Her ambitions, her internal disequilibrium, the irresponsibility of her rulers all made it most improbable that she would not react aggressively out of fear. The naval strategy had not worked, the magic formula of colonial disputes had not continued to embroil Britain with France and Russia. Now this most reluctant and ill-assorted combination was to be welded together by Germany's own unaided efforts.

II

With the making of the Anglo-Japanese Alliance came the moment when tensions which were primarily the result of long-term changes in the nature of the state and the scope of international politics began to interlock with more precise strains within Europe. Their combined effect began to destroy the Concert system.

The Concert had already been sapped by the refusal of the powers to operate some of its mechanisms in the face of the pressures that have been discussed above, and from 1895 onwards it had sustained serious injury from the persistent crisis in the Far East. The effect of the temporary alleviation of the Chinese question after Russia's defeat by Japan in 1905 was to breathe new life into the Near-Eastern problem and to revive Austro-Russian conflict. It has been seen how difficult it was for Bismarck to contain the eastern question, and what subtle gyrations his policies were forced to assume for the sake of German security. When he departed his system was allowed to decay; the more easily because while Germany began to build a High Seas fleet, abandoned the treaty with Russia, changed her relationship with Austria–Hungary and saw the making of the Franco-Russian Alliance, Russia had abandoned the Near in favour of the Far East. If there was one factor which gave reality to Germany's assertion of 'world policy', it was the Austro-Russian agreement of 1897. This agreement upheld the status quo in the Balkans making both a nonsense of the Franco-Russian Alliance, and protecting Germany from the threat of Austro-Russian conflict. When that situation changed after 1905, Germany found herself faced once again with Bismarck's problem, but without the protection which he had arranged. Worse than that, she found herself faced with the consequence of her own actions.

For it was around the turn of the century that actions such as the sending of the telegram to President Krüger of the Transvaal, the seizure of Kiaochow, the whole bombast of Navy League propaganda and the tone in which 'world policy' was conducted began to give rise to suspicions that Germany was a power whose intentions were as reminiscent of Napoleon as her strength. For the first time since 1815 there existed a power which had lost international confidence in its willingness to obey the principles of the Concert, let alone continue to support the efforts of others to replace its mechanism with the brittle security of purely defensive alliances. Nor was this all. Before the situation in Europe had begun to deteriorate noticeably, the first 'impossible' agreement had been made in the shape of the Anglo-French *Entente* of 1904; and Germany had tried to destroy it by staging a serious crisis over Morocco.

The path to the Anglo-French *Entente* began at the Fashoda crisis. In March 1897, the French had despatched Colonel Marchand from Brazzaville in French Equatorial Africa with a small military force to make a demonstration on the upper Nile in the Sudan. He travelled through the Belgian Congo with the connivance of King Leopold and eventually arrived at Fashoda, which was the site of an old Egyptian fort, in July 1898. Unfortunately for him, the implied challenge of his expedition was nullified by its arrival in the Sudan simultaneously with the army of General Kitchener fresh from its great victory at Omdurman. There could be no doubt that, however severe the crisis was, the French would have to withdraw and Delcassé, the French Foreign Minister had no hesitation in doing so in November 1898. The expedition had been designed to offer a threat – albeit a distant one – to Britain's occupation of Egypt and thus force her to negotiate. French policy had always wanted some settlement of the Egyptian question and a resumption of the 'liberal alliance', but their terms were too stringent, and their strength insufficient to force Britain's hand. The Fashoda crisis merely confirmed that this was the case.

But the crisis had two other important effects. It convinced an influential wing of the French expansionist *parti colonial* that an accommodation with Britain must be found, and Egypt forgotten about, in the face of a new need to be ready to cope with the impending collapse of the regime in Morocco. Secondly, the danger of war which the crisis brought had indicated that the Russians were not prepared to operate the Franco-Russian Alliance in Africa, and induced in the French Admiralty an acute realisation of their inability to fight Britain. Delcassé wrote that the decision to withdraw Marchand followed from the 'necessity of avoiding a naval war which we are absolutely incapable of carrying on even with Russian help'.[27] The consequence was an attempt to remove sources of dispute with Britain, so as to reduce the danger of war, but not to abandon Egypt. There were several bridges yet to be crossed before Delcassé would adopt the conclusion that his only course was to seek an agreement with Britain on her terms.

That this situation ever came about was due in large measure to his failure in getting support for firm action which would clear Britain out of Egypt, and his increasing fear of the intentions of Germany. In 1899, the Franco-Russian Alliance was refurbished and the result was not only to make clearer provision for a possible conflict with Britain, which might have been expected, but also to reassure Delcassé that the alliance also existed to secure the balance of power in Europe. His conviction that the German navy represented a grave threat came even earlier than the similar British realisation and he was quick to couple it with other manifestations of German waywardness: he concluded that Germany desired to dismember the Habsburg Empire and become 'a *central* and *universal* power'.[28] Rumours of a *rapprochement* between Germany and Russia persisted, however, particularly during the Boer War, which naturally contributed to French anxieties; but what was decisive for France was the growing suspicion that Germany had shifted her objectives and was, by 1903, contemplating domination of the western Mediterranean through interference in Morocco.

The coming of the Boer War and the reverses which Britain suffered produced both the argument that the moment was obviously right for a settlement with Britain on advantageous terms while she was preoccupied in South Africa, and the counter argument that this was precisely the moment not to seek an arrangement, but to go ahead with more vigorous plans. To this end, Delcassé sought and achieved an agreement with Italy, by which Italian ambitions in Libya were exchanged for French ambitions in Morocco, and the possibility of an Anglo-Italian agreement was thus blocked. The effect was also to protect France from the effects of Italian membership of the Triple Alliance since the Italians now assured them that they would never apply its terms to France. He also came very close to making an agreement with Spain by which Morocco was to be partitioned between them, and other powers excluded. He did not succeed because the Spanish were rightly alarmed at the possibility of British objections to a treaty which had been made without them concerning an area where their trade was worth £20 million. So far did their alarm extend that they leaked the negotiations to Britain in the hope of forcing the French to admit them to the Franco-Russian Alliance.

Nothing, however, was so important in changing Delcassé's attitude towards the idea of an agreement with Britain as his experiences with Germany during the Boer War. The suggestion of an intervention against Britain was mooted from several quarters, not least Russia, and negotiations proceeded in 1899 and 1900 between Germany, France and Russia. The upshot was that the French discovered more of an intention to come to an agreement with Britain on the part of Germany, than a serious resolve to intervene. Certainly the Germans were not really prepared to intervene. They encouraged the idea in the hope of convincing the British that they must accept German terms for an alliance, and to that end they revealed the existence of French designs in London. The result was that in the end they neither obtained French goodwill nor an agreement with Britain. Indeed, when it became clear that the Germans were asking Paris for a reaffirmation of the Treaty of Frankfurt in exchange for discussions of an anti-British coalition, they contributed decisively to changing Delcassé's policy. To learn that they must publicly surrender the lost provinces of Alsace-Lorraine for the sake of an agreement about which they suspected the German government was not sincere, finally undeceived the French. Delcassé refused thereafter to negotiate with the Germans, and in doing so laid the foundations of the first Morocco crisis of 1905.

The way was now open, if Delcassé could be converted to the idea, for an agreement with Britain which would exchange Morocco for Egypt.

Paul Cambon, the ambassador in London, was early convinced that this was the right policy, and he made several moves on his own account with Lansdowne which enabled him to trace and report upon the change in the British attitude. The pressure which had been exercised on Delcasse by some French politicians, ever since Fashoda, to make an agreement with Britain now moved from the private to the public field. At last, in January 1903, Delcassé himself became convinced that Britain was prepared to change her policy. She had hoped for years that the government of Morocco would be able to stand up of its own accord, which, under Mulay Hassan, it appeared likely to do. His death in 1894 and the succession of a minor gave rise to thoughts of 'reform' under British tutelage as disorder spread. It also made the French determined to obtain what was for them a strategic interest of the first importance. Only when the breakdown of the Moroccan government made Fez seem to the French as important as Cairo did the *Entente* become possible; only when the British showed that they were quite willing to abandon Morocco did Delcassé see the chance of a bargain. The British were in fact quite relieved: 'We may', said Lansdowne, 'in our secret hearts congratulate ourselves on having left to another power the responsibility for dealing with so helpless and hopeless a country.'[29]

What finally convinced Delcassé that Britain was ready to come to an agreement was the attitude of King Edward VII and the editor of *The Times*, both of whom were regarded with exaggerated respect on the continent, and both of whom had come to support strongly the idea of a French *Entente*. Their attitude was backed up also by the rising tide of anti-German feeling in Britain. Hatzfeldt wrote that 'The Anglo-French *rapprochement* is the product of a common aversion to Germany ... Without the estrangement of England and Germany a mood of anglophilia would have been impossible in France.'[30] This process had begun at the time of the sending of the Krüger telegram, which elicited an outburst of anger which was inappropriate to its significance. The friend-ship which the Kaiser displayed during the Boer War stemmed the growing tide of hostility in the press, but could not wholly eradicate the feeling that Germany was not pursuing a straightforward policy. The failure of the attempts to secure an Anglo-German alliance between 1898 and 1901 caused the flood gates to open and from then on, fanned by the flames of the Venezuela affair, the mood in England became abusively anti-German. 'The English draw nearer to us,' wrote Cambon, 'in proportion as they feel the hostility between their country and Germany grow and become more acute.'[31] He might have added that the same effect was felt in France. The failure of their negotiations with Germany during the Boer War, coupled with their fear of an Anglo-German *rapprochement*, made them the more ready to seize the moment of intense British discontent with Germany to initiate discussions of their own.

All these developments coalesced at the moment of Edward VII's state visit to Paris in the summer of 1903, where he not only secured a personal triumph but also began negotiations with President Loubet; and when the President of the Republic came to London with Delcassé in July 1903 the French Foreign Minister was able to begin at once by proposing the barter of Morocco for Egypt. The British Cabinet unanimously agreed to pursue discussions. Ironically they were pushed on both by Consul-General Cromer's pressure from Cairo, and by the danger to India from a new railway which the Russians were building to Tashkent – with French money and at Delcassé's urging. Cambon and Lansdowne began detailed negotiations in October 1903, and by March 1904 the task was nearly done. On 8 April 1904 the Anglo-French *Entente* was signed. At one stroke the Egyptian problem was solved and a series of disagreements all over the world were settled up: an apparently fundamental condition of international politics was changed. The centre of gravity was returning to Europe, and this agreement looked suspiciously like clearing the decks.

Almost at once, the new *Entente* was put to the test. One of its purposes was to alleviate the risk to France of a Russo-Japanese war. While the negotiations were in progress the war broke out, and shortly after they were successfully concluded the Dogger Bank incident brought Britain and Russia to the verge of war. Delcassé's efforts to mediate were brilliantly effective, and he earned the gratitude of both the governments. Both agreements were preserved at a moment when the Germans were counting on the breakdown of at least one. Had the Russians won the Japanese war, France would have found it hard to preserve her two agreements, for the British must have tried to prevent Russia from gaining too much in China and it would have ill-become France to obstruct her ally. As it happened, the Russians began to lose and the Franco-Russian Alliance looked like being strengthened by Delcassé's welcome attempts to bring about a negotiated peace. That the outcome of this dangerous crisis should be the strengthening of both the Anglo-French *Entente*, following the Dogger Bank incident, and the Franco-Russian Alliance, on the conclusion of peace, was more than German nerves could tolerate. At least one of the reasons which lay behind her sudden intervention in the affairs of Morocco was the desire to be rid of Delcassé before this result could ensue.

The other reason was derived from Delcassé's refusal to open negotiations with Germany before implementing the *Entente Cordiale* in Morocco. He was in receipt of constant advice to the effect that Germany would not allow herself to be excluded without prior negotiation, and until he was gradually worn down by German pressure he persisted in his refusal to discuss the matter with Berlin. His attitude became alarming, particularly to the Prime Minister, Rouvier, as it appeared that France was in no state to resist a German attack. In February 1905 the first public indication of German intentions emerged in the form of a warning from the German minister in Morocco. In the following month, Bülow forced an extremely fearful and unwilling William II to visit Tangier. In circumstances which, if they had not been so ominous, would have been farcical, the Kaiser asserted before the assembled diplomatic corps that Germany regarded the Sultan as the ruler of an independent state. There was now no avoiding an international dispute nor an international impression that Germany was largely responsible for it. Delcassé at last began to approach the Germans, albeit indirectly, and by April he had spoken on his own initiative to the German ambassador. As April turned into May, Delcassé was strengthened in his belief that the indications of support both official and unofficial which were coming from Britain showed that his firm attitude was correct and that the Germans would eventually give way. His Prime Minister, however, grew ever more fearful of the threat from Germany and by private contacts offered to dismiss Delcassé in the hope of warding off the danger. As the chances of Delcassé becoming the successful mediator in the Russo-Japanese War increased after the Battle of Tsushima, the Germans began to insist that he go. Rouvier now showed reluctance, but the German ambassador finally informed him that so long as M. Delcassé remained in office there was no possibility of an improvement in Franco-German relations.[32] On 6 June 1905 Delcassé duly resigned. It did not come as a shock to him, for through the interception of German telegrams by the Quai d'Orsay he knew both of Rouvier's original offer and of the recent German insistence. Despite the possibility of a great success in his forthcoming mediation, which might have put the presidency within his grasp, despite the chance to silence criticism, he never published the information which would both have saved his office and caused the Germans to change their codes. It was better for France to know what the Germans were doing, than to retain his services; Dr Andrew has written: 'Nothing in his term of office became him like the manner of his leaving it.'[33]

The result was not as comforting as Rouvier had hoped. Bülow was made a prince, but Germany continued to demand a conference on the Moroccan question, despite Rouvier's offer of a comprehensive settlement of outstanding questions. After a further threat, however, he yielded on the conference. The question was now internationalised, and the German government had exchanged the uncertainties of a conference for certain gains at French expense. This error was not even justifiable on grounds of internal policy. *Weltpolitik* was quite as well served by an imperial arrangement with France as by a showy conference.

The conference met at Algeçiras in January 1906, and despite the expectations of Germany the chance of separating France from her allies was not rendered easier by the new Liberal government in London. Sir Edward Grey, the Foreign Secretary, was personally a supporter of the *Entente*, and his instructions to the British delegate were the same as Lord Lansdowne's would have been. Nor was he less than frank with the German ambassador whom he informed that a German attack upon France would not find Britain neutral. Furthermore the military discussions which had taken place in 1905, and which had helped to sustain Delcassé's confidence, were placed on a regular footing, though secret and specifically 'noncommittal'. The opening of these military conversations marked an important change in British foreign policy, for they showed clearly for the first time how far the chief centre of international politics had returned to Europe. Grey had previously held office during the period of acute hostility with France and Russia and recorded how disagreeable it had been to rely upon German support. Moreover, his party had urged agreement with France and Russia while in opposition. He now found himself in a situation where the old imperial preoccupations of British policy had to be sacrificed for the sake of the security of the European system – indeed, to some extent already had been by the French *Entente* – and that meant a new concern with the possibility of military intervention on the continent. The British fleet did not as Rouvier remarked 'run upon wheels', and the thought of military commitments was anathema to the more radical members of the Liberal Cabinet. The result was that Grey had to keep open the possibility of intervention – which could only be done by planning in advance – while refusing to give any formal guarantee to France. The conversations achieved this end, but having no political significance, as he supposed, did not need to be revealed to those who would be alarmed by them. Coupled with persistent warnings to Germany, this was certainly the best policy that Grey could pursue. His hands left technically free, even after the Russian convention, he was able to follow the policy that he afterwards described as going to every length to prevent war, while putting Britain in the best possible position if he should fail.[34] After the first Morocoo crisis, thoughts of European war dominated foreign policies, imposing new and uncomfortable criteria.

The effect of the conference at Algeciras was no less unfortunate. No one wished to deny that Delcasse had been extremely unwise to leave the Germans out in the cold, since Germany had been a signatory to the Madrid Convention of 1880; and they had hoped that the possession of such a good case would automatically secure their victory over France. To make wholly certain they adopted a deliberately confusing policy by which, alternately, the conference was favoured with displays of masterful ill-temper, and the European capitals with siren songs of more than usual dishonesty. The mood of the conference began to shift noticeably towards France and eventually, after the Germans had forced a lengthy deadlock over the question of the police, the British delegate, Sir Arthur Nicolson, secured a vote. The result of this vote was a public demonstration of German isolation: she was defeated by ten votes to three, and she was deserted by Italy. Apart from one more outbreak of ill-tempered tactics, which was induced by Rouvier's resignation from the Quai d'Orsay, the German delegation showed from then on a desire to find quick compromises and wind up the disastrous conference. But the damage was done. A future British ambassador to Russia and Head of the Foreign Office, Sir Arthur Nicolson, was converted to an anti-German viewpoint; confidence in the European system had been seriously shaken; in Britain, it was the inspiration for one of the most influential pieces of analysis ever written by an official of the Foreign Office, when Sir Eyre Crowe set out to show that Germany might be seeking European hegemony.[35] Above all, the whole affair had the effect of strengthening the *Entente* between Britain and France. The British had been as good as Edward VII's word. 'Tell us', he had said, 'what you wish on each point and we will support you without restriction or reserves.'[36] The crisis had also served to change the nature of the agreement. In the face of the German challenge, it was now regarded by both parties as a necessity for their own security. During the conference Grey wrote: 'an entente between Russia, France and ourselves would be absolutely secure. If it is necessary to check Germany it could then be done.'[37] In April 1906 negotiations were begun with a view to making the second 'impossible' agreement – with Russia.

The Anglo-Russian convention of 1907 was certainly a more unlikely agreement than the French *Entente*. The hostility of many members of the British Liberal Party was inevitably directed against the autocratic dictatorship of the Tsar, and their opposition was only increased by the rapid resumption of autocracy after the reforms of 1905. Thus in the middle of negotiations with the Russian government Sir Henry Campbell-Bannerman, the British Prime Minister, declared: '*La Douma est morte: vive la Douma*',[38] and his effusion was only one of many that at this time held up negotiations, and were later to raise frequent doubts about the viability of the Russian *Entente*. The objections of liberal democrats in Britain were paralleled by objections in Russia coming from the military and from nationalist groups, who resented the proposed abandonment of ancient claims. More solid doubts could be found also on both sides. The Russians, who were much weakened by their defeat at the hands of the Japanese, were particularly anxious not to offend Germany, with whom their conservative sympathies so clearly lay. Nor were they anxious to provoke a sequel to the first Morocco crisis, which might follow a new agreement with Britain, as that had followed the French *Entente*. In Britain the 1905 Revolution brought doubts as to the stability of the Russian regime which the ambassador, Nicolson, could allay only by pointing out that if a successful revolution did occur, the resulting regime would be so profoundly different that the whole policy would have to be reconsidered. Meanwhile, it would not help to show doubts about the Tsar's government at the moment when they might be most grateful for an expression of confidence. Finally the sheer extent of the differences which the two powers had must not be forgotten. From China to the Straits they had become traditional opponents, and it was at least as difficult for the government of India to abandon their prejudices as it was for the Russian general staff. If both had not been cajoled by their own colleagues, the chance of agreement would have been wrecked.[39]

Nevertheless, after many months of negotiations, the agreement was signed on 31 August 1907. What factors combined to overcome the difficulties? Britain, as we have seen, had been trying to obtain a settlement with Russia for some years – certainly since 1895. Sir Edward Grey entered office with no less strong a conviction that a Russian agreement was desirable, and it was reinforced by his preoccupation with the balance of power in Europe. He at once indicated his impatience to 'see Russia re-established as a factor in European politics',[40] and with the assent of his colleagues sent Sir Arthur Nicolson to St Petersburg to arrange an *Entente*. If Grey was anxious to re-establish Russia as a great power, the Russians, after their crushing defeat and internal revolution, were no less anxious to be re-established. Their defeat also had the effect of removing the most potent area of Anglo-Russian discord in the Far East. The Russians and the Japanese soon achieved a working partnership and the new position stabilised Russian advances at an acceptable point: there was now no reason why Russia should not come to terms with the ally of Japan. Furthermore, in November 1906, the British gave the first direct hint to the Russians that they might have changed their attitude over the Straits question. For the new Russian Foreign Minister Isvolski, who was vain, ambitious and anxious to prove that a liberal foreign minister could do quite as well as a conservative, this hint was of profound significance. He did not recognise that the Straits were of little importance to Russia at this time, nor did he take sufficient account of the reserve with which the British mentioned the subject. It was left that if the convention proved successful, and therefore popular, the Straits might be discussed. Isvolski was soon to regret that he had taken this to mean that Britain would now welcome a conference on the question. Nevertheless, the preparedness of Britain to go even this far in negotiations – the new position was already privately decided – gave to the Russians a concession from Britain which previously they had lacked. In return for such shadowy hints, support within Russia could be found for an agreement which embraced the problems of Tibet, Afghanistan and Persia, and in which Russia was asked to make some painful reappraisals.

The settlement in Persia was to become a most thorny issue. The Russian zone contained Teheran the capital and her influence, based upon an occupying military force, was correspondingly large. Her agents in Persia were not subject to strict or consistent control from St Petersburg, and it is impossible to deny that the Russians failed to honour the terms of the agreement. It is equally impossible to deny that the British suffered little from this except as a matter of honour, as their zone continued to be the intended protection of the Indian frontier. In this connection, the rage and fury of the radical wing of the Liberal Party knew few bounds, and Grey soon came to abhor the indignities of Question Time. When the Russians dismissed the Persian Parliament by force and installed their own regime, Grey was forced to threaten resignation in the face of a storm of protest. Its authors, in the nature of things, could not know or appreciate the enormous lengths to which he had gone in attempting to moderate policies at St Petersburg. He even said on one occasion that he should perhaps resign in favour of a man who would make an agreement with Germany.[41]

This remark contains within it both the chief reason why Grey withstood successive outbursts against the Russian convention, and the chief reason for its making in the first place. The Russians, for all their softness towards Berlin and for all their greater sympathy with the conservative views that prevailed there, had come to feel that, in Count Witte's words, 'the foreign policy of Germany was so erratic, so impulsive and so eminently selfish', that Russia must not be 'cajoled by the allurements which emanate from Berlin'.[42] These sentiments were given added point by a danger that became a sort of counterpoint to the negotiations. The Russians and the British became convinced that the Germans were attempting to insert themselves into the area of the Persian Gulf, so as to be able to create a new Moroccan crisis if the two powers made an agreement. The scare was not ended by the convention, and in 1913–14 it recurred, once again to the benefit of the Anglo-Russian agreement. For Britain the need to make economies in the defences of India was dictated to some extent by traditional liberal sentiments but, as Grey was frequently to point out in defence of the convention, one reason why it was urgently necessary and why Persian troubles must be swallowed for its sake, was the impossibility of carrying a European and Asiatic burden at the same time. The European burden was compounded both of the possible danger of a continental war and of the race in naval armaments: in both cases the originator of the anxiety was Germany.

The Anglo-Russian *Entente*, completing as it did the arrangements which were begun in 1894, was not a pleasant event for the German government. It was very far from being an offensive weapon against them: it was not even an alliance. But it had been brought into being by a sense of insecurity, and by a desire to buttress the balance of power. To the extent that it did that, and given the preoccupations of German policies and the pressures that lay behind them, it was correct for the Kaiser to minute that 'it is aimed against us'.[43] The Russians had been assured that the agreement was specifically not directed against anyone. If the German government had pursued policies of moderation, it could certainly have prevented the loose agreements of powers surrounding her from solidifying into anything like an encirclement. It was not Germany but the European system that was being taken into care; only if Germany's fears and ambitions led her into more violent outbursts would she herself be imprisoned.

Further Reading

L. Albertini, *The Origins of the First World War* (Oxford: OUP, 1952).

C. M. Andrew, *Théophile Delcassé and the Making of the Entente Cordiale* (Macmillan, 1968).

I. Geiss, *German Foreign Policy, 1870–1914* (Routledge and Kegan Paul, 1977).

J. A. S. Grenville, *Lord Salisbury and Foreign Policy* (Athlone, 1964).

C. H. D. Howard, *Splendid Isolation* (Macmillan, 1967).

W. L. Langer, *The Diplomacy of Imperialism, 1890–1902* (New York: Knopf, 1951).

G. Monger, *The End of Isolation* (Nelson, 1963).

A. J. P. Taylor, *The Struggle for Mastery in Europe* (Oxford: OUP, 1957).

6. The Road to War, 1907–14

The international situation was now beginning to be weakened by the machinery which had been designed to strengthen it. Despite the disclaimers that were written into the various treaties and understandings, the uncertainties which followed from a Liberal government in London, and the duplicities practised by Italy, the international system had lost valuable flexibility. The solution of every crisis had become, it is true, more urgent, but it had also become more difficult. The consequence was that the Concert of Europe, already battered by long-term developments and by the behaviour of Germany, began to fail. It was dangerous enough for doubts to be raised about the health of the European balance, but efforts to achieve security had the effect of returning European quarrels to an insecure Europe, and this at a time when both Germany and Austria were approaching moments of acute internal crisis. With hindsight it is clear that the situation gave little ground for hope that catastrophe could be avoided. Restraint and restraint alone could now save the Concert from destruction: neither of the central powers was for much longer capable of restraint.

Almost at once the making of the Anglo-Russian convention was followed by painful evidence of this fact, and a crisis ensued which might have been a rehearsal for 1914. In 1908 Austria–Hungary annexed the two provinces of Bosnia and Herzogovina. She had had the opportunity to do this in 1878 but, not wishing to incorporate more Slavs into the empire, annexation had been rejected in favour of administration. Thus in 1908 Austria had ruled the provinces for sixty years and, since they were ruled from Vienna rather than Budapest, ruled them well. But they remained under Turkish sovereignty, and technically subject to recall by Constantinople.

In 1908, the Young Turk revolution occurred in Constantinople, which looked as if it might succeed in replacing the faltering autocracy of the Sultan, Abdul Hamid II with something more modern and reformist. The powers, who had just failed to cope with new outbreaks of rebellion in Macedonia, could not but regard this development with pleasurable anticipation. The resurgence of Turkey might solve the eastern question once and for all. For Austria, however, it represented a different and disagreeable prospect. Moderate men were being replaced in Vienna by successors who believed that the only way out of the monarchy's difficulties was by some desperate stroke in foreign affairs: something that would both end the *Ausgleich* and solve the south Slav problem. Goluchowski was replaced by Aehrenthal, who came to the Foreign Ministry from the St Petersburg embassy, and Beck was replaced by Conrad von Hötzendorff as chief of staff. A long-standing advocate of war as a purgative solution in its own right, Conrad particularly favoured a war with Serbia.[1] This was not the moment, therefore, to contemplate the possibility of being asked to surrender both the monarchy's shop window for the Slavs, and its base for future movement southwards, to a refurbished and reformist Turkish government.

Disturbances in the Balkans were bound to interest the Russians more after 1907 than for many years hitherto. The war with Japan, and the agreement with Britain had reduced Isvolski's scope for pursuing successful policies to the point of confining him to the Balkans. The Austrians now rightly believed that Germany would support their every action, if not out of sentiment, then because they had no choice. Russia now possessed two friends, and the possibility of Austro-Russian conflict in the Balkans was also the possibility of European war. Aehrenthal thought that he could manage Isvolski, and Isvolski thought that he might use Austrian desires to force a conference on the Straits question, at which he now believed he would have the support of Britain.

The two ministers met at Buchlau in Bohemia, in September 1908, where some such bargain was evidently discussed. It is not known precisely what passed at this Ruritanian meeting, except that Isvolski certainly thought that both the annexation and the Straits would have to be submitted to a conference, and that Aehrenthal was to follow this policy if Isvolski could arrange for it to meet.[2] In years gone by, Isvolski would have been wholly correct. But it was now Aehrenthal's intention both to resist a conference and to bring off the annexation. Almost immediately after the Buchlau meeting, the annexation was declared, and Isvolski was left high and dry in Paris, apparently duped by the Austrians and disowned by his own government, who no longer cared about the Straits. Left without support for his schemes, Isvolski then fell back on the idea that there should be a conference on the annexation alone, at which he hoped to restore his and Russia's prestige. Aehrenthal, who had not informed the Germans of his plans, now fell back upon their support. Their initial reaction had been most unfavourable. Having spent years building up their influence at Constantinople, it was galling to observe their ally dissipate their efforts with one stroke. But they soon came to believe that Austria must be supported because, as Von Bülow said, Russia had joined Britain and, which did not necessarily follow, must therefore be humiliated.[3] The chance seemed to be there, for neither Britain nor France wished to be involved in a war over the Balkans and if they did not support Russia, the Triple *Entente* ought to be severely shaken. It was the Algeçiras of the Anglo-Russian *Entente*.

When the conference, despite Grey's support, failed to come off, and the French refused to back Russian demands for compensation for Serbia, it was clear that Austria had the chance to snuff out Serbia altogether. Aehrenthal would not seize the opportunity, out of dislike for the increase of Slavs that the annexation of even half Serbia would bring to the monarchy, and contented himself with making Belgrade acknowledge what had been done. The Germans decided that Russia must also be made to acknowledge it and that if possible, Isvolski, like Delcasse, must be made to resign. In March 1909 the German government asked Russia to acknowledge the annexation and 'for a precise answer – yes or no – ', failing which they would allow a war to follow.[4] Whether this was a disguised ultimatum or not – and there has been much discussion of the issue – the Russian government supposed that it was. They gave way and, indeed, Isvolski was eventually removed from his post; but the consequence was a strengthening of their resolve, an increase in their forces, and the injection of an anti-German element into the Triple Entente. In 1914 German backing went to Austria as before; but a German ultimatum to Russia had the opposite effect. Above all, the length of the crisis and the manner of its solution devalued yet further the principles of the Concert.

The general situation was not improved by a marked decline in Anglo-German relations which set in after 1909. The Bosnia crisis itself had a disagreeable effect upon most members of the British government, an effect which was only confirmed by the outbreak of sharp exchanges between the two countries over naval matters. This development changed the focus of European politics and for the first time brought Britain clearly to the centre of things. It was from this time that Anglo-German hostility seemed to be the primary issue and caused the British Foreign Office to adopt a firmer attitude towards the preservation of the *Ententes*. Since this hostility, particularly after the bad scare which the Agadir crisis caused, also produced a demand in both countries for a *rapprochement*, there grew up a curious dichotomy of approach in which fundamental suspicions would allow neither country genuine concessions with which to woo the other.

The naval conflict had been born with the German Navy Bill of 1897, weaned with that of 1900, and finally came of age with the invention of the Dreadnought. The Germans used all sorts of arguments to justify their fleet, ranging from the protection of commerce to the 'general purposes of our greatness'.[5] The construction of a High Seas fleet was both a popular policy in its own right and associated with the pursuit of a world policy. Its first purpose had been to force Britain into dependence upon Germany by threatening her naval supremacy through concentrating the new German fleet in the North Sea. This policy could only work if it was not coupled with *Weltpolitik* and Britain was carefully prevented from gaining other friends. In fact, as has been seen, Britain did find other friends, and she was not intimidated by the prospect of having to outbuild Germany at sea. Once the policy of securing British alliance by threats had failed, it would have been better to abandon the large navy, use the raw materials and manpower for the construction of continental weapons and thus avoid a needless quarrel with Britain. But the navy could no more be abandoned than world policy. Its part in German life was too vital, its support from the Kaiser too persistent and in the end the German government had to accept the possibility of war on two fronts at the same time as war at sea. (See chapter 3.)

They were not unaware of their peril. The most striking avowals of fear and weakness can be observed at intervals from those who had embarked upon a quest for world power. The ambitions of post-Bismarckians did not so much replace the fears of Bismarck as overlay them. Whenever Germany was approached by any of her 'rivals', she always sought for an alliance, or for declarations of neutrality. This was partly because she did not wish to be hindered in realising her ambitions, but partly out of fear. At one moment of extreme Anglo-German discord, the Kaiser remarked that all would be well if only he could have an alliance with Britain like her alliance with Japan. But German terms were always too closely binding to entice powers who had become deeply suspicious: indeed the very rigour of German offers only increased their unease.[6]

The British had begun to be worried about the German navy in 1901, but only to the extent of being determined to keep the advantage that they already had. After the invention of the new and more destructive

Dreadnought in 1906, both navies found themselves in possession of largely obsolete warships. The race was therefore now on more open terms, and a naval crisis was an immediate fact. In November 1907 the Germans tried to take advantage of the new situation, and of British moderation in their estimates, by introducing a new bill into the *Reichstag*. The British countered with increased estimates in March 1908, and steeled themselves for more. Simultaneous naval reductions were suggested, and at once the basic issue obtruded itself, as it was to do during all naval discussions from 1908 to 1913. The Germans would only offer a reduction of the building rate, or a slowing of its tempo, if they could have very definite assurances of British neutrality, or an alliance, in return. The British, who were more interested in economies, retorted that the Germans would not need to make such demands if they enjoyed the goodwill that would follow from a reduction in naval building. Besides which, the British had decided not to abandon the *Ententes* – although they came perilously close to doing so in 1912 – for fear that 'we shall eventually be attacked'. They would come only to a technical naval bargain; the Germans would make only a political agreement.[7]

The question attracted public notoriety at the same time as the Bosnia crisis reached its peak, when the British suspected, perhaps wrongly, that the Germans had tried to steal a march on their parliamentary estimates by laying down two extra Dreadnoughts. Tirpitz subsequently offered explanations, and certainly only the contracts were let; but the consequence was a conviction, not only on the part of British officials, but also for the first time on the part of the public at large that the Germans had tried to do them down. The public outcry brought new and enlarged estimates, and an increase of bad feeling. It also brought the suggestion from Grey that to prevent such a crisis recurring, there should be exchanges of naval information. Discussions on this point followed from 1909–11, when they were interrupted by the Agadir crisis. But they were no more successful than a resumption of direct negotiations on the naval race, which were pursued with the new Chancellor, Bethmann-Hollweg. An attractively liberal figure, he induced confidence in the representatives of foreign powers. But the vacillations of German policy soon convinced them that his control over policy was defective, and the admirable effect which he produced was dissipated by the entirely correct suspicions that in the last resort Bethmann-Hollweg would not be able to stem the tide within Germany. And he, too, for the sake of his prestige with the *Reichstag* needed a political agreement above all else. Deadlock continued, and the ships continued to roll down the slipways.

Discussions were abruptly halted in July 1911 when the Agadir crisis broke upon one of the hottest summers of this century. The crisis was caused by the same problem as the first Morocco crisis of 1905, and unfortunately led to a similar result. The French had gradually extended their influence in Morocco after the Algeçiras Act of 1906, and were clearly about to take the final step of inaugurating a protectorate. The decision at Algeçiras would undoubtedly have been contravened by such an occurrence, if indeed the extension of French influence had not already done so. Thus the Germans would have had a good case for seeking negotiations for a resettlement of Morocco, and probably compensations for themselves, had it not been for the existence of the Franco-German convention on Morocco of 1909. By this, Germany had agreed to disinterest herself politically in Morocco in return for economic concessions. They had decided nevertheless to warn the French in April 1911 that the departure of troops for Fez would cause them to abrogate that convention. It is clear that the Germans wanted to force a West African colony out of the French in return for consenting to their occupation of Morocco. It is equally clear that the French Prime Minister, Caillaux, desired to achieve a settlement by this method, and throughout the crisis he negotiated privately with the German government along these lines. The matter was taken out of the hands both of Caillaux and of the German Foreign Secretary Kiderlen-Wächter, by the means which the Germans employed to get their way. It was evidently Kiderlen's intention to present to the French a threat of such magnitude as to make it easy for them to hand over the French Congo without seeming to have betrayed the French nation to the point where they would take on Germany in Europe. A German warship, the *Panther*, was therefore stationed off the south Moroccan port of Agadir and, by being there, violated the Algeçiras Act, threatened the French position on Morocco and suggested the danger that she might retain the port for a naval base. The weapon was infinitely too large for the purpose and the result was an Anglo-German crisis which was quite the most serious before 1914.

It is possible that, as was his wont, the Kaiser had returned from a recent visit to Britain convinced of the inalienable goodwill of the British people and thus, as was also his wont, had concluded that it would be safe to threaten the Anglo-French *Entente*. Whatever the reasons for the sending of the *Panther*, the British at once exhibited great concern. Grey was willing to send a British ship to Agadir also, but was overruled by the Cabinet. He informed the German ambassador, however, that 'we could not recognise any new agreements which might be come to without us'.[8]

The Germans failed to reply to this for twenty days, and in the meanwhile began direct negotiations with France, in addition to those which Caillaux was already engaged upon. On 21 July the Chancellor of the Exchequer, Lloyd George, spoke at a Mansion House luncheon and gave public notice in unequivocal terms that Britain would not tolerate being left out of negotiations where her interest was at stake. His speech gave a new air to the crisis. He was a well-known radical, who might be thought to be an influence for peace – almost at any price – and his threat of war was both colourful and precise. On 25 July the German ambassador at length broke his silence, to such effect that Grey had to warn the Admiralty that the fleet might be attacked at any moment. Through August and early September the crisis deepened, and from 8 to 22 September Britain put discreet preparations for war into effect; from July the French and British armies possessed the details of military co-operation. The war clouds began to disperse when, possibly as a result of a financial crisis in Germany, the Germans began to climb down and by November an agreement had been signed. France received a recognised position in Morocco, and Germany received some parts of the French Congo.[9]

The consequences of the crisis were, however, not so quickly absorbed. The independent negotiations which Caillaux had been having with Germany became known and he was forced from office. He was replaced by a Lorrainer, Raymond Poincare, who spoke in different tones and took up the new mood which infected France after the Agadir crisis was over. It was a mood of confidence, and it was a mood that boded no good to German schemes for detaching France from her friends. Perhaps by virtue of Poincare's different attitude to Russia, his arrival in office (first as Prime Minister then as President of the Republic) was one of the more damaging gifts which the Germans presented to themselves. Equally damaging in a different way was the appointment of Winston Churchill to the British Admiralty. The army had recently been successfully reformed under Lord Haldane, and the Agadir crisis revealed that the navy was sorely in need of a similarly improved organisation. To give the task to Churchill was to silence a hitherto radical voice and an intimate colleague of Lloyd George. He was turned into an indefatigable supporter of the navy, and his chief suspicions, like the navy's own, soon became directed at Germany.[10]

The chief outcome of what Grey described as 'this fit of political alcoholism' was an increase in general anxiety.[11] For the first time for half a century two European powers had shaped up to one another with war as an expectation. The Germans had gambled for the first time with a policy which could only be rationally based upon a threat of war. They had not prepared for it, because their policy was not rationally based; British policy was, however, and countered the threat with genuine preparations. Public sympathies became involved; there was public humiliation in Germany, public anxiety in Britain and a national revival in France. There was probably little real danger of war; but there was thought to have been, and such violent policies and counter-policies breached a large hole in the security of the powers and the viability of the Concert.

After the Agadir crisis of 1911, there was again an attempt to secure an Anglo-German *détente*. It took the form of direct negotiations about the navy and a political agreement conducted by Lord Haldane; there were also renewed negotiations about the Portuguese colonies, following from the convention of 1898. The improvement that was thought to have come from these was assisted by an agreement reached about the Baghdad railway, as part of a general settlement with Turkey in the Persian Gulf area. Moreover in the period between Agadir and the outbreak of war, the German government behaved with considerable circumspection during the Balkan Wars, which were thus prevented from causing a general crisis. The consequent improvement in the tone of Anglo-German relations was very far from being another lost opportunity. It was a false calm which must not be allowed to obscure the fact that Lord Haldane's mission failed for exactly the same reasons as other negotiations had failed, despite a British attempt to meet German terms which went beyond anything that they had previously considered. The result was that the really serious issues between the two countries were not again discussed before 1914. Both sides indicated that they did not wish to discuss the naval question any further, because it brought only ill-feeling in its train. The British did not again propose political settlements to the Germans after they were categorically told in 1912, in the aftermath of Lord Haldane's mission, that only a declaration of unconditional neutrality could induce them to come to any sort of agreement with Britain. The convictions of the British Foreign Office became more clearly anti-German than at any previous time – to such an extent that Grey was forced to go outside his own department in order to make any gestures that might appease his radical colleagues. Officially the book was closed in March 1912 and discussions of serious issues ceased.

The negotiations over the Portuguese colonies, which were taken up with energy in 1912 in an attempt to loosen some of the rigours of the

Agadir crisis, were conducted both unofficially and officially, and ultimately ended in a most revealing failure. They were not intended to be a primary issue. The hope of those who believed in them was that they would, if successful, induce a generally more satisfactory atmosphere in which more important things could be done. They could usefully be referred to as 'current negotiations' and they absorbed the attentions of radical ministers who might otherwise have damaged the *ententes*. The result was that after much painful and laborious discussion a new territorial settlement was worked out, by which Germany was the gainer, to go into operation if the Portuguese Empire fell apart. The Germans had always felt cheated of their inheritance when the agreement of 1898 had not been quickly followed by the collapse of the Portuguese Empire. Indeed, it is clear that they supposed that the two beneficiaries would kill off the aged relative as soon as possible. Instead, they rightly suspected, the British had contracted agreements to protect Portugal and had every intention of postponing for as long as possible the day on which the agreement would come into force. The same difficulty applied to the revised agreement. The new territorial provision, having taken two years to arrive at, was allowed to lie fallow until it was rendered null by the outbreak of war. The Portuguese colonies negotiations, conceived to ameliorate Anglo-German relations in a relatively unimportant area, failed because the Germans insisted that the conventions affecting Portugal made by either side might not be published before coming into effect. The paradoxical reason for this was that publication of an agreement made to improve relations would cause such an outcry that any improvement as there had been would be lost.[12]

The Balkan Wars, which occupied the anxious attentions of statesmen in 1912 and 1913, produced the last example of the Concert in action. They seemed to provide a quite inevitable cause for a general war: the interests of Austria were at issue; the Straits were at issue; the alliances and *ententes* appeared to ensure that if Austria and Russia should fight, the war must spread. But instead, the great powers were able to unite sufficiently to bring the warring Balkan states to an ambassadors' conference in London. Although many disputes were settled there the conference could not prevent the outbreak of a second round of fighting, which was fortunately so decisive that the crisis was not long enough to lead to disaster. This was true also of the first Balkan War. The success of the Balkan allies against Turkey was so rapid and so complete that after only a few weeks it was no longer an issue whether Austria and Russia should quarrel over the formation of a new territorial settlement in the

Near East. So far was this true that Russian policy, hidden though it had to remain, became much concerned to prevent the Bulgarians from actually taking Constantinople. Their position was such, as Isvolski's enterprises had shown, that they were not strong enough to contemplate the general opening of the Straits. They wanted the Turks to stay and thus preserve Russian isolation in the Black Sea. This was the more necessary, and contributed markedly to French policy, in that Russian loan repayments in grain and her industrial imports were flowing through the Straits, and any dislocation would bring disaster. The Turks, however, saved Constantinople for themselves and thus prevented the Straits from becoming an issue.[13]

With the major problems for Austria and Russia already pre-empted in one way or another, it was a most fortunate feature of the crisis that in the early stages the German government would not allow itself to be drawn to Austria's automatic defence. The reasons for the conciliatory behaviour of the Germans were twofold: in the first place, Bethmann-Hollweg still believed that he could obtain a political agreement with Britain, and that the chances of doing so would be much increased if Germany assisted in a settlement by the Concert. In the second place, an overwhelming argument in favour of moderation came from the military, who were strongly opposed to going to war in what they considered to be the wrong place and at the wrong time. The latter was the most important point. German military preparedness would reach its height in the autumn of 1914, and this fact became clearer after Bethmann-Hollweg passed an army bill through the *Reichstag* in March 1913. The temptation in 1914 would be very great; in 1912–13 it was resistible, and the more so if Bethmann-Hollweg could use the opportunity to detach Britain from her friends.[14]

Although the result was a striking tribute to Grey who had taken the chair at the London meetings and to the conference method itself, the whole affair left behind uncomfortable tensions. In the later stages of the crisis, the Germans had not hesitated to urge their support upon Austria. Possibly this was because they knew that she no longer wished to fight against the Balkan League or in that situation at all. Nevertheless, their offers made a deep impression upon Berchtold, the Austrian Foreign Minister. In October 1913, for example, the Serbs had crossed into the new state of Albania – created in deference to Austrian wishes, to hold up Serbian expansion – in the hope of quelling guerrilla attacks. The Austrians sent an ultimatum, which had its due effect, and drew support from the Kaiser: 'You can be certain I stand behind you and am ready to draw the sword whenever your action makes it necessary . . . whatever comes from Vienna is for me a command.'[15]

Expressions of support for Austria from Germany were, for the first time, paralleled during this crisis by expressions of support for Russia from France. Poincaré, who had come to power in France as a result of the Agadir crisis, took a different attitude towards Russia from his predecessors. It was partly to do with the new belief of the French general staff that they could defeat Germany in war, and partly to do with the enormous financial interest that France had by now acquired in Russian industry. It was also partly to do with Poincaré's own determined character. He did not hesitate to tell the Russians that France could not go to war just for Russian interests in the Near East; but, contrary to previous French practice, he emphasised both the fact that German intervention would automatically bring France to Russia's aid and that such intervention was very likely. For the Russians, whose feelings about the Straits had prevented them from following their usual policies towards their fellow Slavs, the hints were important for the future. If a crisis arose in which the issue was much clearer cut, they could have a new confidence in the Franco-Russian Alliance.[16] On this occasion, the powers had with much difficulty permitted an ambassadorial conference to regulate the results of the war. This was because the crisis was indigenous to the Balkan states themselves, and only involved the powers at one remove; because Austria and Russia were content to see it so; and because Germany had seen no advantage in exacerbating the situation. But Serbia was much enlarged, which alarmed Austria, despite her success in creating Albania; Bulgaria was diminished after the second outbreak, which showed how much the Russians had allowed Slav interest to go by default. If a new crisis arose in which Austria and Russia were involved directly, they would not be likely to be able to resist their respective desires to destroy and defend Serbia. Nor, it is clear, would their allies restrain them again or the European system have the strength to endure.

Further Reading

L. Albertini, *The Origins of the First World War* (Oxford: OUP, 1952).
V. R. Berghahn, *Germany and the Approach of War in 1914* (Macmillan, 1973).
F. Fischer, *War of Illusions* (Chatto & Windus, 1975).

I. Geiss, *German Foreign Policy, 1870–1914* (Routledge and Kegan Paul, 1977).

F. H. Hinsley (ed), *British Foreign Policy under Sir Edward Grey* (Cambridge: CUP, 1977).

Z. S. Steiner, *Britain and the Origins of the First World War* (Macmillan, 1977).

A. J. P. Taylor, *The Struggle for Mastery in Europe* (Oxford: OUP, 1957).

7. The Moment of Collapse, 1914

The assassination of Francis Ferdinand on 28 June 1914 was not at first thought likely to develop into a major crisis, at least by the standards of the preceding years. Some perhaps uncharitable relief was generally expressed that the manifold embarrassments caused by the late Archduke would cease,[1] and it was widely supposed that there would have to be some retributive action taken against Serbia. At an early stage, and without the possibility of the proof that was later to be so searched for, there was a general assumption that Serbia was partly, if not wholly, responsible for the assassinations. Even in Germany there was no initial recognition that a final crisis was beginning, though this may have been in part because some of the principal actors in the German government were away, or just about to go away, on their summer holidays.

Thus it is difficult to see in the event itself a crisis fundamentally different from the many others that occurred between 1900 and 1914, particularly since one of the worst of them – the Bosnia crisis of 1908–9 – presented so similar a threat of Austro-Russian, and thus Russo-German, conflict. There were, however, some noticeable differences. In the case of the Bosnia crisis, Russia had been seeking gains at the Straits, gains which not all Russians regarded as vital. In 1914 the status, perhaps the very existence of Serbia appeared to be at stake. On this point there was no doubt of a widely supported Russian determination. At the end of the Bosnia crisis, Russia was forced to back down over her opposition to the annexation of the provinces by the thinly veiled threat of force from Berlin. So soon after her defeat in the Russo-Japanese War, and the subsequent domestic rebellion, Russia could not have gone to war. By 1914 the recovery of Russia, in all respects, had become a significant cause of German anxieties. Furthermore, in 1908–9 there was some doubt as to the cohesion of the Triple Entente, particularly as to how far the French and British governments would go in supporting Russia. In the event of a continental war, it was not clear whether Britain could, or would, intervene militarily across the channel; and certainly the French, both in policy and in military preparations, did not seem ready to face a war. ,By 1914 successive emergencies, particularly that of Agadir in 1911, had caused the British to prepare for intervention in Europe, and to embark upon quite large-scale military and naval co-operation with France. If it remained uncertain whether Britain would join a continental war, there was no longer any doubt that she could do so if, at a particular crisis, intervention were to become her policy.[2] Again, after 1911 the *réveil national* and the vigorous presidency of Poincaré gave a real point to the newly energetic military measures that the Agadir crisis eventually induced. By July 1914 the Russians had no reason to think that their ally would let them down, indeed quite the reverse. And, even the British connection which had seemed to be under so much strain, because of intense disagreements about Persia, was strengthened by the Anglo-Russian Naval Agreement of 1914.[3]

These considerations alone, however, do not explain the outcome of the assassination crisis. The Balkan Wars of 1912–13, although initiated by independent states at one remove from the great powers, raised many of the same difficulties for Austria and Russia that both the Bosnia crisis and the final crisis had or would raise. Yet it was possible, though not without great strain, for a version of the conference method to be applied and, up to a point, to succeed. It is difficult, therefore, to identify any single simple factor which made the difference in 1914. There is, however, a sense in which it is not necessary to do so. The habits and customs, the apparently natural limitations of policy which had so much characterised the preceding century, were not and had not become an irreversible part of the conduct of international politics. They were the result of certain conditions and, although through inertia they might survive a change in conditions for a bit, it was plain that sooner rather than later habits of restraint would become impossible to maintain. What was not certain was the pace of change and therefore the exact moment at which the Concert system would collapse. Nor was it certain that, when it did collapse, it would collapse into a great war. From German evidence it would appear that their military calculations suggested that after 1916, it would no longer be advisable for German policy to risk war.[4] From the evidence of the Balkan Wars, and perhaps some other signs, it does not appear certain that the European system would have collapsed within two years. It was not inevitable that adjustment to a new distribution of power could only come through war.

A combination of events was needed to achieve the result of 1914.

First, the steady erosion of the mechanism of the Concert of Europe needed to have reached the critical point. Second, German policy needed to retain and sharpen the willingness to risk war that had become its characteristic since 1905. Third, the response of other powers needed to be such that would accept the risk posed by Germany and turn risk into reality. In practice this meant that Russia should decide to resist, and that Britain should support France. Finally, the opportunity for this combination had to occur and that, in the conditions of 1914, meant a crisis involving Russia in eastern Europe.

The opportunity, arising in the shape of the assassinations at Sarajevo, is not difficult to explain. There lay behind it a long history of insensitive Magyar rule in the south Slav areas of the monarchy, and a consequently frustrated Slav nationalism. (See chapter 3.) It was perhaps an unfair irony that the expression of that frustration should have occurred in the one part of the monarchy where south Slavs were ruled from Vienna rather than Budapest. By a similar irony, it was the peculiar status of the provinces of Bosnia and Herzogovina that made them attractive to the Archduke Francis Ferdinand: only there could his wife be afforded the full honours of protocol, elsewhere denied her because of her insufficiently aristocratic origins. That the monarchy should run into incidents created by nationalist feeling was inevitable, given the conflict between nationalist aspirations and the Habsburgs; that the situation in south-eastern Europe should be noticeably more difficult was also inevitable given the arrangements of 1867, and the aftermath of the Balkan Wars, the one involving recognition by Serbia and the other raising the vexed question of Serbian access to the Adriatic; there could be no doubt of the likely involvement of Serbia in any incidents that might occur. Thus it is strikingly easy to see why a crisis might develop between Austria and Serbia. What its outcome might be depended on other factors.

The first of these – the erosion of the mechanism of the Concert of Europe – has been the subject of much of the preceding chapters. There were profound changes taking place in the distribution of power and the government of states, and these developments had by 1900 removed the basis upon which the European system had rested. Thereafter it was clear that crises came more quickly, increased in number and were progressively harder to solve. After 1911 the threat of war became an accepted feature of the stage on which foreign policies were conducted, as it had not been since the Napoleonic Wars. At any time therefore unless some fundamental readjustments to new conditions occurred, the diplomatic mechanism might collapse. In such circumstances, very small events can bring about catastrophic results and yet be impossible to identify. There is an enormous and largely unsuccessful historiography which has attempted to achieve proof at this level, and it would not be productive to try again.

There has also been, in recent years, an astonishingly thorough and able examination of German policy by German historians. They have been convinced that there was a general crisis in Germany, which has been described in depth, and that this crisis had a consistent effect upon German foreign policy both before and during the 1914 crisis itself. As has been seen, many of the difficulties surrounding the rise of Germany had recognisable domestic causes. The rise of a great working class, the development of huge conurbations, the establishment of great trades unions led to the growth of social democracy and the most powerful Social Democratic Party in Europe. The position of Prussia, the position of the monarchy and the existing constitutional arrangements were all threatened by this change in the social structure of the Reich, and no group more so than the Prussian agrarian élite. With this group no kind of uneasy compromise could be made. The existence of powerful forces on the left might make the middle classes easier to handle through their fear of socialism, but socialism itself was unappeasable. The consequence of this was the appearance of a shaky coalition of shifting elements, made up of the old agrarian groups, the new industrialists, ship-owners and bankers and a scared bourgeoisie. This conjunction of interests, to a greater or lesser extent, supported the imperial government in seeking and operating policies which were designed to detach or distract the working classes from the SPD. Because the industrial revolution had both destroyed the social cohesion of the Reich and given it very great international power, these policies tried to use the latter to cure the former. A traditional response of Bismarck to the appearance of political difficulties had been to produce a foreign scare. His successors responded by illustrating sharply the potential threat that Germany had become to others by adopting a vehemently 'nationalistic' foreign policy; and when that produced an unfavourable result internationally, used the consequent and quite genuine fears to conjure once again a domestic cry of 'danger'. Both these manifestations were designed to relieve internal domestic pressures.

This then was the base from which German foreign policy came to be conducted. In the absence of a 'legitimate' and accountable government, the machinery of administration was controlled by a changing coterie of the Kaiser's largely reactionary and Prussian friends, whose preoccupation was with protecting their social and political position against the threats posed by the new industrial Germany. For this purpose foreign policy, as it had been for Bismarck, was regarded as an entirely suitable weapon with, by the turn of the century, the added opportunities inherent in the policy of creating a High Seas fleet. So much was this a tradition, and so great was the accumulated fear of domestic instability, that the worsening external situation tended to be ignored until, after 1907 particularly, its strikingly unfavourable condition became in itself a kind of goad.

If there were reason enough for a domestically attractive and nationalistic foreign policy to be found in the unstable condition of politics,[5] there was also not lacking a considerable community within Germany who were urging a forward policy on different grounds. The German academic community, particularly professors of history, were eloquent in their general support for a geo-political and social-Darwinian approach to the analysis of German problems and possible solutions. The former gave grounds for supposing that Germany was becoming, perhaps had become, the most powerful state in Europe, and that therefore she ought to pursue a forward policy and make gains – usually expressed in terms of colonies – appropriate to her power status. This idea was the more easily held in conjunction with the notion that the relationship between states was based on a constant struggle to bring about changes in the distribution of power, and that in this struggle firm resolution on the part of the strongest would wrest gains from those who had been overtaken and were in overt political decline. This amounted to a convenient combination, for in many minds it was both an argument against democracy, or its extension, since that might preclude resolute policies, and at the same time an argument for a vigorous foreign policy. It was this aspect of German opinion, so vigorously and publicly expressed, which impressed foreign commentators greatly at the time, and which seemed to historians for a long time to be the principal domestic motive power propelling German policies.[6] It is clear that the Colonial League and the Navy League both have this kind of background. Sometimes it has been possible to see some German politicians, Bethmann-Hollweg for example, as standing out against this stream in German political and intellectual life.

However compelling the German problem in all its manifestations may seem to be, it is important to keep in mind the vital significance of the general state of international politics as they had developed since the

1870s. As can be seen from Part One, so difficult had circumstances become that it might almost seem unnecessary to offer any additional explanations for the failure of the powers to cope with it, and certainly inappropriate to suggest that any valuable analysis could be added on the basis of the actions of states or individuals. At times in the extensive historiography of the subject, this has been an attractive conclusion to arrive at.

On the other hand, the great weight and authority of recent German historical work has made such a conclusion seem too deterministic.[7] It has also, perhaps not deliberately, had the effect of obscuring the importance of the long-term factors which were eroding the fabric of the Concert of Europe. It must be kept in mind that it was only the context of international affairs that could give Germany the desire to seek world-power status, whether as an essentially long-term defensive policy, or more simply as a short-term and relatively local aggression of a traditional kind. Moreover, it should be pointed out as well given the particular weight often allowed to this factor, that it would not have been possible for German governments to have conceived of foreign policy as a weapon in the domestic struggle if the international situation had not been as it was. And not until after the turn of the century was Germany herself anything like a principal contributor to the character of that situation.

Thus it can be seen how essential it is to balance the factors that have been discussed. There were two simultaneous shifts occurring in the distribution of power: one moving slowly on a world scale in favour of the United States and Russia; the other moving rapidly but locally in favour of Germany. These interacted, and they did so at a time when other strains were following from changes in the nature of power and the practice of government. The progress of technology provided the motive power for many of these changes and contributed to others, particularly in armaments, and in widening the disparity of power between the developed areas of the world and those less developed. Superimposed upon these factors, and in some ways a consequence of them, lay the very important problems of Germany and the Habsburg Empire, and once the distribution of power had decisively changed in Germany's favour, the effect of these problems projected into international affairs seemed to become a dominating factor. But in the light of what has been discussed, it is difficult to see the particular difficulties of Central Europe as undisputed prime movers in the history of the breakdown of the Concert of Europe. To understand it, however, requires the longer and wider view, allowing neither the primacy of the German situation nor the primacy of the 1914 crisis itself.

In this last lies a peculiarly likely source of confusion. By the summer of 1914 most of the damage had been done; there was very little leeway left for compromise or manoeuvre. Through all the obscurities of the sometimes hectic diplomatic action, it can be seen that Germany at least could not accept an outcome, whether by war or not, which did not bring a substantial and public victory for her and her ally. Some of her leaders would have preferred not to go to war, and the contradiction between that feeling and that fact that they eventually did so adds to the impression of German irresponsibility that the crisis gives. By then, however, the essential confusion of German policy was confronted by a positive response from the other European powers. For Germany to attain security in Europe, to achieve world power on the basis of parity with the British Empire, the United States and eventually Russia, and to bring about a permanent amelioration of domestic policies were not compatible aims of policy. Their incompatibility had produced increasing confusion in German policy after 1900, particularly after 1907, and was to produce the sense of being trapped which marked her behaviour during the final crisis. The truth was that these aims of policy were only compatible in the context of war, and during the crisis of 1914 the truth emerged.

In 1914 this confusion was quite evident.[8] The German reaction to the assassinations was strikingly inconsistent. To begin with, it seems clear that the German government wanted Austria to act quickly and without warning against Serbia. They wished to gamble on the possibility that international recognition of the enormity of the crime would allow rapid retribution to pass without causing the resulting crisis to spread. There began therefore to be a stream of encouraging communications from Berlin to Vienna in the hope of pushing the Austrians into an action which would gain an overwhelming success for the Triple Alliance without leading to war. But the incitements of the German government, in part derived from their own domestic preoccupations, ran into trouble in Vienna because of Austrian – or more strictly Hungarian – domestic considerations. It had never been the wish of the Hungarians after 1867 that a great foreign success should accrue to the monarchy; it had also been their wish that no increment of Slav nationals should further aggravate the national problem – particularly in the Kingdom of St Stephen. For them, therefore, the response to the assassination crisis was one of great caution and Tisza, the Hungarian Prime Minister, was able to prevent any kind of precipitate and unannounced action against

Serbia of the kind proposed by the German government. Inevitably the longer that action was postponed, for whatever reason, the less possible it became to present war for international and domestic German consumption as a just and natural retribution.

First because of Hungarian doubts, and then because of the calculated intention to deliver an ultimatum to Serbia after rather than during a state visit by Poincaré to St Petersburg, the response became more and more delayed. That there should be one ultimatum was agreed to by the Hungarians on 14 July – a full ten days after the first German proddings had arrived – and its final text was agreed on 19 July. Even then it was not to be delivered until 23 July, after the German government had received a copy on 21–2 July.

After the delivery of the ultimatum on 23 July at 6 pm, German policy changed. What had been first a determination to propel Austria into rapid action and then to secure a suitably rigorous ultimatum, became a more complicated policy of protecting Austria from attempts at mediation by the powers. This policy involved a greater risk of war – a risk accepted by Bethmann-Hollweg from the beginning – and therefore involved a new element of preparation. For Germany it was desirable but, at least in military and naval circles, not expected that Britain should remain neutral for as long as possible. It was even more desirable that a divided and tense home society should universally accept any war as having been forced upon Germany by others. There was a noticeable preoccupation with this factor, bearing as it did upon the willingness of the SPD to vote war credits in the *Reichstag*, and upon civil order and military morale. For this purpose, it was essential that, if the crisis was going to lead to war, enough time should elapse for the Russians, whose mobilisation period was significantly longer than that of other powers, to be forced into some action which would justify the German government in setting their own war machine in motion.

Thus for the moment the German government merely forwarded without comment to Vienna attempts to persuade them to draw the Austrians towards mediation. When on 27 July Grey proposed a conference of ambassadors, the German Chancellor replied that Germany 'could not bring Austria–Hungary's dealings before a European tribunal'.[9] Despite urgings from other powers that Vienna could and should accept the Serb reply as a great victory, Austria declared war on Serbia on 28 July.

At this point, the handling of the crisis in Berlin began to move out of the Chancellor's, and indeed civilian, hands. Amidst growing evidence that the newly declared conflict could not be kept local, German policy changed again and its main thrust was to make Russia appear the initiator of war. This would allow the irreversible military measures which Moltke and his staff were now insisting upon to be begun in a manner acceptable to German public opinion outside the ruling groups. How important this was, and what confused reactions it could lead to, were clearly to be seen in the extraordinary exchanges of 28–9 July. Bethmann-Hollweg had become by now fairly certain what the outcome was going to be and remained convinced, as the soldiers were not, that it was still worth playing for British neutrality. He therefore offered Britain a pledge that, in exchange for neutrality, there would be no destruction of France in Europe. Grey subsequently described this proposition as a disgrace,[10] but even before he knew of it he had warned Lichnowsky in London that Britain might well not be neutral. In the light of this evidence of Grey's attitude Bethmann-Hollweg became greatly alarmed at the use Britain might make of this offer in relation to France. He at once sent urgent restraining notes to Vienna – the first and the last of such a character – in order to fend off the possibility of war beginning in circumstances which might cast suspicion on the German government. This was the reason for an otherwise inexplicable turn-round of policy, as was revealed when it was sharply reversed on receipt of the first news of Russian war preparations which reached Berlin in the course of the night of 29 July. Nor was it necessary to preach restraint to Vienna. At this point, as earlier, the Austrian government was still seeking to extricate itself from its own dilemmas without inducing widespread conflict. On 29 July Berchtold and Shebeko – the Russian ambassador at Vienna – were engaged in bilateral discussions, and this after Russian partial mobilisation had been confirmed. However, on 31 July at 12 noon Russian general mobilisation was announced.

With that declaration, the German government had succeeded in waiting for the moment of greatest political advantage. The war could now begin, as General von Waldersee later said, 'by itself'.[11] After lunch, the pre-mobilisation order was signed and the process of gathering in allies, or hoped-for allies, was begun. On the next day the general mobilisation formally began, and later in the day Germany declared war on Russia, which Austria was not to do for another week. In the days following, Germany declared war upon France and then, after the invasion of Belgium, Britain declared war upon Germany. The risk of war, which had become an integral part of German policy, was now an actuality.

There was no doubt that a fundamentally Austrian crisis had turned into a German war. It was Germany who was relying upon the support of Austria in a war with Russia, and it was a war which Germany had declared in response, ostensibly, to Russian mobilisation. Why did Russia go thus far in the Serbian crisis, when she had not on earlier occasions, particularly during the Bosnia affair? Part of the answer is that in 1914 Russia was for the first time since the 1905 Revolution able to dare a firm response. That this was so stemmed both from her greater political stability, and from the enormous strides which her economy had been making since the late nineteenth century. This last factor had become much more obvious in the years just before 1914 and was in itself one of the reasons why some Germans at least foresaw a conflict with her as inevitable. It was also true that while Russo-German relations avoided any nadir during the Balkan Wars, they had none the less been conducted in a steadily worsening atmosphere in the year before the outbreak of general war. The most persistent example of this was the highly aggressive tone of press comment upon the Tariff War then going on. The most frightening example however was the Liman von Sanders affair in 1914 itself when the Russians objected strongly to the appointment of a German general to command the Turkish army in the Constantinople district. Both gave to the Russians a sense of alarm about German intentions which, coupled with their (temporary) naval disadvantage *vis-à-vis* the Turkish fleet in the Black Sea, gave them a highly defensive attitude.[12]

In these circumstances, it was not surprising that as the assassination crisis became more alarming, the Russian government began to worry about the need for (at least) a partial mobilisation. For Russia, as the German government well knew, the process of mobilisation was extremely slow and cumbersome. It could not and did not have the same significance as mobilisation by any other of the European great powers. Even so the Russian government, particularly the Tsar, was reluctant to embark on mobilisation, and it is plain that only the invasion of Serbia caused the Russians to mobilise the districts immediately facing Austria on 29 July. The German government responded to this by itself threatening to mobilise which, in view of the fact that the response was very much more serious than the initial stimulus, amounted to a hidden ultimatum. Again, despite the shelling of Belgrade which seemed to show that the Germans either could not or would not restrain Austria, the Tsar refused to consent to a general mobilisation because the Kaiser had sent him a conciliatory telegram. Eventually, however, the conviction grew that Germany was not in fact conciliatory, that war with Austria must be followed at once by war with Germany, and that therefore the dangers of not making mobilisation general were equal or greater than those of restraint. In the afternoon of 30 July the Tsar signed the order for general mobilisation. For the German government, as has been seen, this action provided the finishing touch to the scenario in which they intended to press the crisis to a conclusion. For the Russians, it was an essentially preventative gesture, which was accompanied by a further attempt to find a solution by direct talks with Vienna. Bethmann-Hollweg did not think Russia wanted war: 'Although Russia had proclaimed a mobilisation its mobilisation measures could not be compared with those of other western European (powers) . . . Russia did not want war, it had been forced by Austria to take this step.'[13]

The Russian mobilisation need not have led to war, but in the circumstances of German domestic politics particularly, it was essential for Bethmann-Hollweg's policy that Russia should oppose the German threat at least thus far. That she did so helped to make 1914 different from preceding crises in that it offered an opportunity to Germany which had previously been lacking.

The question of why Britain entered the war in support of France is comparatively easy to answer; in the event it was because the invasion of Belgium, in defiance of the European guarantee of neutrality which Belgium enjoyed, united almost completely a British Cabinet which might otherwise have been seriously divided. It is an ironic commentary that while some Germans – Bethmann-Hollweg for example – believed deeply in a policy of trying to secure British neutrality in the event of war with France and Russia, the military did not share their view and through the revised Schlieffen plan made quite certain that any efforts in that direction would fail once a war began and Belgian neutrality was violated. But there remains the fascinating speculation about what British policy would have been if Germany had not entered Belgium, or had consented to confine the war on the eastern front with Russia alone, assuming the French would have remained quiet in such circumstances. It looks very much as if the answer is that the British government would have been unlikely to support Russia, if she remained alone. It also looks as though public opinion would have forced the Cabinet, if not immediately then very soon, to support France if she were attacked by Germany. The grounds would not have been that Britain was committed to doing so: British policy had been careful to avoid any binding commitment, although it is impossible to deny that military conversations, the Anglo-French Naval Agreement of 1912 and a steady succession of nods and winks added up to a moral obligation. The ground would have been that which Edward Grey was prone to employ when remonstrating with the German government: that the British had come to fear that the Germans meant to crush France in order to alter the balance of power in Europe, and that if the British government permitted this to happen, it would only have to intervene later to reverse the effects of a French defeat.[14] If it had not done so it is difficult to believe that Grey and indeed Asquith himself would have remained in office. In the event, the German government solved the dilemmas of the London Cabinet for them and at a stroke justified all those policies which had at least given the British the chance to intervene effectively in Europe if they so decided. This was the final outcome of the Agadir crisis in 1911, the real consequence of the *Panther*'s leap.

At 2 pm on 4 August 1914, the British government despatched an ultimatum to Germany asking to know by midnight whether, as the French government had done, the German government would give an assurance that they would respect the neutrality of Belgium. No answer came and at midnight therefore the British Empire joined the war. But it was not yet at war with Austria, nor indeed was Austria at war with Russia, so far into the background had the assassination itself retreated. At this moment it was clear, as at no previous point, that it was not the chain of events from the murder of the Archduke to the outbreak of war that had been decisive. A much longer chain, involving great shifts of power, fundamental changes in the nature of power itself, the expansion of the scope of international politics, had led to the destruction of the European international system: the Concert of Europe had at length collapsed.

World politics could not be conducted by what was purely a European comity of states, nor with preconceptions about international practice derived from the relationship of Cabinets in the middle of the nineteenth century. New problems, new objectives, a new scope, all combined to introduce an element of uncertainty into the system. The atmosphere of mutual trust disappeared first, but the diplomatic if not the conference machinery survived until the shocks caused by the crises after the turn of the century gradually destroyed the confidence which had been its chief virtue. If it is important to observe that internal crises in two great states interlocked with severe international tension in 1914, it is no less important to note that it was also at this moment that the Concert of Europe finally collapsed. It might have come sooner, or a few years later: the destruction of confidence is too intangible a process to be minutely observed. It actually occurred during the stress of the assassination crisis and thus completed an unprecedented interlocking of conflicting interests. The outcome was an appalling conflict, some of whose causes rendered both the First World War and its sequel of 1939 irrelevant to the mainstream of international politics. The future lay no longer in Europe, and the 1914 war was a world war only in the sense that Germany fought for world power. The correct forecast which gave rise to such ambitions contributed much to some thirty years of internecine conflict. This of itself ultimately quickened the process of European decline.

Further Reading

L. Albertini, *The Origins of the First World War* (Oxford: OUP, 1952).

V. R. Berghahn, *Germany and the Approach of War in 1914* (Macmillan, 1973).

I. Geiss, *July 1914* (Batsford, 1972).

H. W. Koch (ed), *The Origins of the First World War* (Macmillan, 1972).

Z. S. Steiner, *Britain and the Origins of the First World War* (Macmillan, 1977).

List of Principal Dates

1870	Franco-Prussian War
1871	Unification of Germany
1873	First Three Emperors' League (*Dreikaiserbund*)
1876–8	Near-Eastern Crisis and War (Russia, Austria, Italy)
1878	Congress of Berlin
1879	Austro-German Alliance
1881	Second Three Emperors' League
1882	Triple Alliance (Germany, Austria, Italy)
1884–6	Partition of Africa
1884	Berlin Conference (Congo)
1885	Near-Eastern Crisis (Bulgaria, Russia, Austria, Turkey)
1887	Reinsurance Treaty (Germany, Russia)
1890	Dismissal of Bismarck
1894	Dual Alliance (Russia, France)
1895	Trans-Siberian Railway completed
1895	Treaty of Shimonoseki (Japan, China)
1895	Triple Intervention (Germany, Russia, France: Japan)
1896	Krüger Telegram
1897	Seizure of Kiaochow (Germany)
1897	First German Navy Bill
1898	Fashoda Crisis (Britain, France)
1898	The Hague Conference (Disarmament)
1898	Portuguese Colonies Agreement (Britain, Germany)
1899	Hay Circular (United States about the Far East)
1900	Yangtse Agreement (Britain, Germany)
1901	Last attempted Anglo-German Alliance
1902	Anglo-Japanese Alliance
1903–5	Russo-Japanese War (Russia defeated)
1904	*Entente Cordiale* (Britain, France)
1905	Revised Schlieffen Plan (for a German attack upon France through Belgium)

1905	First Morocco Crisis (Germany, France)
1906	Algeçiras Conference
1907	Anglo-Russian *Entente*
1907	Triple *Entente*
1908	Acceleration Crisis (Anglo-German naval tension)
1908–9	Bosnia Crisis (Austria, Russia, Germany)
1911	Second Morocco Crisis (Agadir)
1912	Lord Haldane's Mission (Britain, Germany)
1912	Anglo-French Naval Agreement
1912–13	Balkan Wars
1913–14	Russo-German Tariff War
1914	Liman von Sanders Affair (Russia, Germany, Turkey)
1914	Anglo-Russian Naval Agreement
1914	Assassination of Archduke Francis Ferdinand

References

(London is the place of publication unless otherwise stated.)

1 The General Context

1. A. C. H. C. de Tocqueville, *Oeuvres complètes*, vol. III (Paris, 1864–6) conclusion.

2. F. H. Hinsley, *Power and the Pursuit of Peace* (Cambridge: CUP, 1963) ch. 8.

2 Outside Europe: Africa and the Far East

1. G. F. Hudson, *The Far East in World Politics* (Oxford: OUP, 1937) chs 5, 6, 7 and 8.

2. W. C. Sellar and R. J. Yeatman, *1066 And All That* (1970) pp. 99–100.

3. M. S. Anderson, *The Eastern Question* (Longman, 1966) ch. 5.

4. J. Ridley, *Lord Palmerston* (Constable, 1970) chs XVI and XVII.

5. A. J. P. Taylor, *The Struggle for Mastery in Europe, 1848–1918* (Oxford: OUP, 1957) pp. 65–6.

6. E. Hertslet, *The Map of Europe by Treaty*, vol. II, 1814–1875 (Butterworth, 1875) pp. 1250–87.

7. Taylor, *The Struggle for Mastery*, p. 294.

8. R. E. Robinson and J. Gallagher with Alice Denny, *Africa and the Victorians* (Macmillan, 1963) pp. 24–5.

9. D. W. Brogan, *The Development of Modern France* (Hamish Hamilton, 1959) p. 217; A. S. Kanya-Forstner, *The Conquest of the Western Sudan, A Study in French Military Imperialism* (Cambridge: CUP, 1969).

10. Taylor, *The Struggle for Mastery*, p. 282.

11. Ibid., p. 277.

12. *Cambridge History of the British Empire*, vol. III (Cambridge: CUP, 1959) p. 119.

13. W. L. Langer, *European Alliances and Alignments, 1870–1890* (New York: Knopf, 1950) p. 296.

14. Taylor, *The Struggle for Mastery*, p. 298.

15. Ibid., pp. 299–301.

16. E. A. Crowe, Memorandum on the Present State of British Relations with France and Germany, 1 January 1907, *The Origins of the War*, vol. III, appendix A. G. P. Gooch and H. W. V. Temperley (eds), *British Documents on the Origins of the War, 1898–1914* (HMSO, 1927) vol. III, Appendix A.

17. Taylor, *The Struggle for Mastery*, p. 293.

18. E. Eyck, *Bismarck and the German Empire* (Allen & Unwin, 1958) p. 275.

19. G. Barraclough, *An Introduction to Contemporary History* (Pelican, 1967) pp. 107–8.

20. C. M. Andrew, *Théophile Delcassé and the Making of the Anglo-French Entente* (Macmillan, 1968) pp. 51–2.

21. Barraclough, *Introduction to Contemporary History*, p. 109.

22. See I. H. Nish, *The Anglo-Japanese Alliance: the Diplomacy of Two Island Empires, 1894–1907* (Athlone, 1966).

23. Taylor, *The Struggle for Mastery*, p. 400.

3 Inside Europe: Domestic Pressures and the Redistribution of Power in Central Europe

1. See A. Ramm, *Germany 1789–1919* (Methuen, 1967) pp. 318–25.

2. H. Böhme, *An Introduction to the Economic and Social History of Germany* (Oxford: Blackwell, 1978) pp. 69–71.

3. J. C. G. Rohl, *Germany without Bismarck* (Batsford, 1967) p. 30.

4. M. Balfour, *The Kaiser* (Cresset, 1964) p. 433.

5. Ramm, *Germany 1789–1919*, p. 377.

6. Rohl, *Germany without Bismarck*, ch. 3.

7. Ibid., chs 4, 5 and 6.

8. Ramm, *Germany 1789–1919*, p. 390.

9. See J. A. Hobson, *Imperialism: A Study* (1902; Allen & Unwin, 1938); V. I. Lenin, *Imperialism the Highest Stage of Capitalism* (1916; Moscow: FLPH, 1947).

10. Ibid., p. 391.

11. J. H. Clapham, *The Economic Development of France and Germany, 1815–1914* (Cambridge: CUP, 1945) ch. XI.

12. L. Cecil, *Albert Ballin; Business and Politics in Imperial Germany, 1888–1918* (Princeton, 1967) p. 212.

13. W. Hubatsch, *Die Ära Tirpitz* (Göttingen, 1955) and G. G. B. Ritter, *Staatskunst und Kriegshandwerk: Das Problem des 'Militarismus' in Deutschland* (Munich, 1954–60).

14. J. Steinberg, *Yesterday's Deterrent* (Macdonald, 1965) p. 26.

15. Ibid., p. 59.

16. V. R. Berghahn, *Germany and the Approach of War in 1914* (Macmillan, 1973) pp. 6–9; M. Kitchen, *The German Officer Corps, 1890–1914* (Oxford, OUP, 1968) pp. 222–7.

17. Steinberg, *Yesterday's Deterrent*, pp. 59–60.

18. Ibid., p. 21.

19. Berghahn, *Germany and the Approach of War*, pp. 15–16.

20. Ibid., pp. 165–9 and p. 186.

21. O. Jaszi, *The Dissolution of the Hapsburg Empire* (Chicago, 1929) parts III and IV.

22. Taylor, *The Hapsburg Monarchy* (Peregrine, 1951) p. 212.

23. Jaszi, *Dissolution of the Hapsburg Empire*.

4 The Role of Technological Change

1. Hinsley, *Power and the Pursuit of Peace*, pp. 264–5.

2. Böhme, *Economic and Social History of Germany*, pp. 87–91.

3. E. J. Hobsbawm, *Industry and Empire, an Economic History of Britain since 1750* (Weidenfeld and Nicolson, 1968) pp. 149–63.

4. F. Fischer, *War of Illusions* (Chatto & Windus, 1975) pp. 379–85; A. Gerschenkron, *Economic Backwardness in Historical Perspective* (Harvard, 1966) ch. 6.

5. See F. H. Hinsley (ed.), *British Foreign Policy under Sir Edward Grey* (Cambridge: CUP, 1977) chs 10, 11 and 15.

6. See E. L. Woodward, *Great Britain and the German Navy* (Oxford: OUP, 1935).

7. H. J. Mackinder, 'The Geographical Pivot of History', *Geographical Journal*, XXIII, 4 (1904); see also Mackinder, *Britain and the British Seas* (Oxford, 1925).

8. Taylor, *The Struggle for Mastery*, p. 56, n. 1.

9. M. J. M. Larkin, *Gathering Pace, Continental Europe, 1870–1945* (Macmillan, 1969) pp. 88–90; *New Cambridge Modern History*, vol. XI, ch. IX (Cambridge: CUP, 1962).

10. Hinsley, *Power and the Pursuit of Peace*, pp. 256–9.

11. Taylor, *The Struggle for Mastery*, pp. 344–5. Hinsley, *Power and the Pursuit of Peace*, pp. 259–62.

12. Ibid., pp. 262–70.

13. S. J. Hemleben, *Plans for Peace through Six Centuries* (Chicago, 1943) pp. 128–9.

5 The Grouping of Powers, 1890–1907

1. The *Spectator*, 29 March 1890; for Bismarck in general, see A. J. P. Taylor, *Bismarck the Man and the Statesman* (Hamish Hamilton, 1955) and Langer, *European Alliances and Alignments*.

2. Taylor, *The Struggle for Mastery*, pp. 329–30.

3. Ibid., p. 328.

4. Ibid., p. 345.

5. Ibid., pp. 339–40.

6. Ibid., p. 336.

7. G. Monger, *The End of Isolation* (Nelson, 1963) pp. 104–7.

8. C. H. D. Howard, *Splendid Isolation* (Macmillan, 1967) pp. 14–18.

9. Howard, *Splendid Isolation*, pp. 75–8.

10. Gooch and Temperley, *British Documents*, vol. I, no 118 and vol. II, no 125.

11. See W. N. Medlicott, *Bismarck, Gladstone and the Concert of Europe* (Athlone, 1956).

12. J. A. S. Grenville, *Lord Salisbury and Foreign Policy* (Athlone, 1964) ch. 2.

13. L. M. Penson, *Foreign Affairs under the Third Marquis of Salisbury* (Athlone, 1962) p. 10.

14. Hinsley (ed.) *British Foreign Policy under Sir Edward Grey*, p. 146.

15. Taylor, *The Struggle for Mastery*, p. 375.

16. W. L. Langer, *The Diplomacy of Imperialism, 1890–1902* (New York: Knopf, 1951) pp. 485–96.

17. Taylor, *The Struggle for Mastery*, p. 343 and n. 1.

18. Langer, *The Diplomacy of Imperialism*, p. 501.

19. Ibid., p. 503.

20. Ibid., p. 504.

21. Ibid., p. 507.

22. Ibid., p. 518.

23. R. T. B. Langhorne, 'Anglo-German Negotiations concerning the Future of the Portuguese Colonies, 1911–1914', *Historical Journal*, XVI, 2 (1973) 361–87.

24. Langer, *The Diplomacy of Imperialism*, pp. 658–9.

25. Gooch and Temperley, *British Documents*, vol. II, no 86.

26. H. W. Koch, 'The Anglo-German Alliance Negotiations: Missed Opportunity or Myth?' *History* (October 1969) 378ff.

27. Andrew, *Théophile Delcassé and the Making of the Entente Cordiale*, pp. 102–3.

28. Ibid., p. 128.

29. Ibid., p. 195.

30. Ibid., p. 205.

31. Ibid., p. 203.

32. Ibid., p. 297.

33. Ibid., p. 301.

34. See K. G. Robbins, *Sir Edward Grey* (Cassell, 1971).

35. H. Nicolson, *Lord Carnock* (Constable, 1930) ch. VII.

36. Ibid., p. 174.

37. Taylor, *The Struggle for Mastery*, p. 442.

38. J. Wilson, *A Life of Sir Henry Campbell-Bannerman* (Constable 1973) p. 535.

39. Hinsley (ed.), *British Foreign Policy under Sir Edward Grey*, ch. 6.

40. G. M. Trevelyan, *Grey of Fallodon* (Longman, 1937) p. 182.

41. Z. S. Steiner, *The Foreign Office and Foreign Policy, 1898–1914* (Cambridge: CUP, 1969) p. 132.

42. Nicolson, *Lord Carnock*, p. 250.

43. Ibid., p. 257.

6 The Road to War, 1907–14

1. See Taylor, *The Hapsburg Monarchy*, ch. 17; also, N. Stone, 'Moltke – Conrad: Relations between Austria–Hungary and German General Staffs, 1909–1914', *Historical Journal*, IX, 2 (1966) 201–28.

2. L. Albertini, *The Origins of the First World War* (Oxford: OUP, 1952) vol. I, pp. 206–10.

3. Taylor, *The Struggle for Mastery*, p. 453.

4. Albertini, *The Origins of the First World War*, pp. 285–6.

5. Hinsley (ed.), *British Foreign Policy under Sir Edward Grey*, ch. 15.

6. Langhorne, 'The Naval Question in Anglo-German Relations, 1912–1914', *Historical Journal*, XIV, 2 (1971) 359–70.

7. Hinsley (ed.), *British Foreign Policy under Sir Edward Grey*, chs 11 and 15.

8. E. Grey, *Twenty-five Years* (Hodder & Stoughton, 1928) vol. II, pp. 37–8.

9. Ibid., pp. 39–45.

10. W. S. Churchill, *The World Crisis, 1911–1918* (NEL, 1968) vol. I, ch. 4.

11. Nicolson, *Lord Carnock*, p. 348.

12. Hinsley (ed.), *British Foreign Policy under Sir Edward Grey*, ch. 15. Langhorne, 'Anglo-German Negotiations . . .'.

13. Albertini, *The Origins of the First World War*, pp. 365–487.

14. R. J. Crampton, 'The Balkans as a factor in German Foreign Policy, 1912–1914', *Slavonic and East European Review*, LV (3 July 1977) 370–90.

15. Taylor, *The Struggle for Mastery*, p. 500.

16. Albertini, *The Origins of the First World War*, pp. 402–18.

7 The Moment of Collapse, 1914

1. See for example, Gooch and Temperley (eds), *British Documents*, vol. XI, no. 19.

2. Z. S. Steiner, *Britain and the Origins of the First World War* (Macmillan, 1977) pp. 189–214; R. Jenkins, *Asquith* (Collins, 1965) pp. 242–5.

3. Hinsley (ed.), *British Foreign Policy under Sir Edward Grey*, p. 255.

4. Fischer, *War of Illusions*, pp. 399–403.

5. See Berghahn, *Germany and the Approach of War*, ch. 8.

6. For example, Professor Theodor Schiemann, Professor of History at the University of Berlin, who contributed a weekly article on foreign affairs to the *Kreuz Zeitung*, in the years before the war.

7. Barraclough, *Introduction to Contemporary History*, pp. 98–9.

8. The details of the July Crisis are most exhaustively treated in Albertini, *The Origins of the First World War*, vols. II and III. More recently, the material has been very successfully re-ordered and published in two volumes edited by I. Geiss, *Julikrise and Kriegsausbruch 1914* (Hanover, 1963–4). The most easily accessible treatment for English readers is to be found in Berghahn, *Germany and the Approach of War*, ch. 12; and I. Geiss, *German Foreign Policy, 1870–1914* (Routledge and Kegan Paul, 1977) ch. 16.

9. Fischer, *War of Illusions*, p. 485.

10. Grey, *Twenty-Five Years*, vol. II, p. 179.

11. Berghahn, *Germany and the Approach of War*, p. 207.

12. Fischer, *War of Illusions*, chs 15 and 16.

13. Ibid., p. 492.

14. For example, Gooch and Temperley (eds), *British Documents*, vol. VI, no. 539.

Index

131